Preachers of Hate

PREACHERS OF HATE

The Rise of the Far Right

Angus Roxburgh

To Neilian, Ewan, Duncan and Catriona

First published in the UK in 2002

Gibson Square Books Ltd
15 Gibson Square
London N1 0RD
tel: +44 (0)20 7689 4790
fax: +44 (0)20 7689 7395
publicity@gibsonsquare.com
www.gibsonsquare.com

UK and European Distribution & Sales by:
Turnaround Publishers Services
Unit 3
Olympia Trading Estate
Coburg Road
London UK N22 6TZ
tel: +44 (0)20 8829 3000
fax: +44 (0)20 8881 5088
orders@turnaround-uk.com
www.turnaround-uk.com

International sales and permissions contact:
Gibson Square Books Ltd in London

ISBN 1-903933-21-8

Typesetting by Triviandum
Printed by WS Bookwell Ltd

Contents

Acknowledgements

For some reason, despite regularly covering the rise of Europe's far right for four years as the BBC's Europe Correspondent, it had not occurred to me to assemble my thoughts on the matter in a book. Doing so has been a fascinating process, allowing me to uncover facets that day-to-day journalism had missed. I should therefore like above all to thank Martin Rynja of Gibson Square Books for suggesting the project, and for his sensible editorial assistance throughout. Thanks too to Susanne McDadd for her indefatigable publicity work.

I am most grateful to Iris Debremaeker for her research, fixing and translation skills. Saskia Stegeman and Dave Shubart helped obtain research materials for me.

Acknowledgements

Faced with such a wide variety of European countries and politicians to consider, I very much appreciate the time taken by the following colleagues to read through individual chapters and offer advice: Bethany Bell, Jamie Coomarasamy, Kerstin Fischer, Claude Moraes and David Willey. All misunderstandings and mistakes that remain are, of course, mine.

My wife Neilian read and commented on the entire book as it progressed, through what was meant to be a summer holiday. My warmest thanks go to her, and to my children, Ewan, Duncan and Catriona, with a promise that I won't do that again.

Preface

February 2000. A new millennium scarcely born. And shivers ran down the spine.

In Vienna, on the edge of the Heldenplatz, where Hitler had saluted an adulating crowd in 1938 after annexing Austria, lines of riot police held thousands of angry demonstrators back from the imperial palace, while inside its elegant walls far-right politicians were once again being sworn in to serve in government. Jörg Haider, the Freedom Party's leader who had praised the Third Reich, stayed away, but his faithful lieutenants were now Austrian government ministers. I tried to broadcast from inside a car, trapped between the protesters and the police, the windows pelted with eggs and paint aimed principally at the police but also knowingly at the press, who had failed, these fearful people felt, to save them from the return of fascism.

That night thousands marched round the city Ringstraße, their breath clouding in the freezing air, banging pots and pans, blowing whistles, and chanting, '*Widerstand! Widerstand!*'

Resistance!

Police used batons and water-cannon to beat back demonstrators who surged through the city's narrow streets and tried to storm the Freedom Party headquarters. Other protestors sat quietly on the lawn outside the palace, nursing their fears in the warmth of a thousand flickering candles.

Away from the anti-Haider protestors, 'vox pops' — the journalist's snatched attempt to gauge public opinion — revealed the nonchalance and credulity of people disenchanted with modern politics.

'There's nothing wrong with Haider. He reduced rents in [his home province of] Carinthia.'

'What does "extreme right" mean? It doesn't exist.'

'Let's give Haider a try. It's time the government listened to the voice of the people.'

'I don't like Hitler, and what he did to the Jews... but he had his good side, I mean, everyone had a job...'

*

Six million murders, but everyone had a job. This was not just historical amnesia, but an appalling reminder of how easily populism can turn into fascism. The dangers inherent in that glib statement would haunt Europe over the next two years, as more and more far-right populists — guaranteeing jobs, a crackdown on crime, an end to a perceived 'flood' of foreigners — gathered millions of votes all over the continent. When Hitler came to power it was all about jobs too, and national pride, and dignity for 'our people'. The Nazis did not start out by gassing Jews: the Holocaust was preceded by a host of 'socialistic' promises for the common man, by the identification of scapegoats, by a campaign of hate, by boycotts of Jewish businesses, and then pogroms like the *Kristallnacht*, when Jewish businesses and synagogues were destroyed, and dozens of Jews killed.

In another part of Europe, Jean-Marie Le Pen was drawing similar equations between jobs and immigrants. Three million unemployed French people equals three million unnecessary foreigners in the country: throw them out and give the jobs to the French. He did not suggest the immigrants should be gassed, but he did incite hatred against them, and he did, chillingly, describe the Nazis' gas chambers as a mere 'detail of history'. In England, the British National Party started a campaign to boycott Asian businesses. In Holland, Pim Fortuyn suggested his country was too full of foreigners. The question was: were these, too, first steps towards something much more awful, something not intended at this stage but capable of growing from the seeds of hatred?

As the millennium dawned messages of intolerance were heard all over Europe — in Belgium, Flemish nationalists poured scorn on the Moroccan community; in Italy, the Northern League leader, Umberto Bossi, threw homosexuals out of his party and foreigners out of the country; even in genteel Denmark, bourgeois populists politely called for Muslims to be expelled, perhaps themselves unaware of the corrosive effect of their lightly-concealed racism.

Meeting the new extreme-right politicians over the past few years has been disconcerting, because outwardly so many of them were perfectly pleasant. They were not the crude skinhead types who terrorised immigrant areas in Britain and Germany (but thankfully held little political sway in those countries). They were articulate, middle-class men and women: engaging, charismatic, colourful, and often remarkably sun-tanned and fit. They were distinguishable from mainstream politicians only by the radical nature of their politics. The message was extreme, but the 'presentation' — from the slick advertising campaigns to the smiling faces of the leaders — was persuasive: designer fascists.

Of course, there were more obviously disquieting moments, too: Le Pen's posturing, the cries of 'Sieg Heil!' from Haider's supporters, Silvio Berlusconi's brazen use of personal wealth to buy power, the march of neo-Nazis through Berlin, and the emergence of assassination as a political tool.

For three years Europe has been mesmerised by the far right. Its successes have appalled and shocked. But they have also changed the direction of mainstream politics — not by encouraging, as one might have expected, a strong left-wing challenge, but by causing centrist parties to move to the right and adopt more populist policies. In Britain, just as I was completing this book, New Labour's policy gurus issued a warning to the party leadership that they had to toughen their stance on immigration (something they had already done) in order to meet the challenge of the far right. They correctly noted that it was the Left's natural constituency among the unemployed, the marginalized and the traditional working class that felt most threatened by immigration and crime — but instead of advocating traditional left-wing solutions such as tolerance and integration, they suggested the way to win back votes from the far right was to copy their policies. One of the themes of this book is that the risk of infection by far-right ideas is as dangerous, at least, as the rise of the extremists themselves.

✶

Writing the book helped me uncover some surprises. I was aware that foreigners and the European Union were the main targets used by the far right to stir up xenophobia and nationalism. I was less aware of the extent to which the extremists' success has also been a backlash against decades of consensus and political correctness in European politics, or of the extent to which Germany stands out as a model of tolerance, keeping the far right in check and avoiding the temptation to take on their policies.

The far right in Europe is not at all homogeneous. It has many manifestations, with different priorities and policies emphasised by the various parties from country to country. The first chapter of the book tries to find the common themes and roots. The following chapters look separately at the rise of the far right in different countries, beginning with Austria and Germany partly because of the Haider phenomenon which first sparked people's fears and partly because of their Nazi pasts, which allow us to examine more closely the roots of today's movements and the continuities that exist between the modern far right and what went before. I then look at Europe's oldest and most pugnacious far-rightist, Jean-Marie Le Pen, at Italy's disturbing trio (the separatist, the fascist and the crook), and at the strange case of Pim Fortuyn. In Belgium I follow the Vlaams Blok on the stump, and in Denmark I fall out with the immigration minister. A chapter on Britain examines why its racist parties are failing to make much impact on voters — but are having an extraordinary influence on government policies. And a further section looks at the rise of ultra-nationalists in eastern Europe. Finally, the book analyses the historical context, asking why the far right made such progress at the turn of the millennium: it looks at the role of Islam and the September 11th terrorist attacks on New York and Washington, examines the Europe-wide swing to centre-right parties since 1999, and discusses the extent to which the mainstream has taken on certain far-right policies — particularly regarding crime and immigration — and how the shift in the European Union's centre of gravity will affect its future. In conclusion, I attempt to draw the threads together and assess how dangerous the new populists are. Is the resurgence of the extreme right in the nineties and early 21st century a blip, or something more worrying and permanent?

1.

Faces of Fascism

Europe only really woke up to the danger in November 1999 when Jörg Haider's Freedom Party came second in Austria's general election with 27 per cent of the votes and went on to take power at national level, with half of the ministerial posts in a coalition government. Until then the extreme right had been perceived as a fringe phenomenon, with nasty but negligible skinhead elements causing localised trouble and political parties incapable of making inroads in Europe's democracies.

Since then it has chipped away like an axe at the complacent heart of that democracy, and in some cases split it asunder. In Belgium the Flemish nationalist Vlaams Blok became the dominant party in the great merchant

21

city of Antwerp. In France Jean-Marie Le Pen crushed a serving prime minister, no less, in a presidential election and went on to the final round of voting. And peaceful, consensus-driven Holland was plunged into crisis when the anti-immigration Pim Fortuyn was assassinated on the eve of a general election but nonetheless swept in posthumously to second place.

Established governments did not seem to see it coming. When electoral success forced them to take notice, there were panic measures — an ill-conceived diplomatic embargo against Austria — and much talk of how these individuals and groups should be defined: were they neo-Nazis or fascists, extreme right, or 'merely' populist? Fortuyn, it was pointed out, was anti-Muslim but not anti-Jewish, as though this somehow exonerated him.

But even now there has been little serious discussion of the causes of their emergence and reasons for their success. Worse, the response of mainstream parties has been to steal their policies, rather than dealing with the factors that make voters resort to far-right groups. In country after country, left-wing governments which were dominant in the European Union in late 1998 have been losing elections. In their place are centre-right coalitions which have either adopted illiberal immigration policies or are propped up by the extreme right. In 2002 Denmark's far-right Danish People's Party, though not a member of the coalition, saw its radical anti-immigration policies adopted as law by the centre-right government, turning the country at a stroke from one of Europe's most welcoming into the most difficult for foreigners to settle in.

*

There are many reasons for what has happened, but the most striking relate to a set of circumstances that took shape at the end of the twentieth century which encouraged a resurgence of nationalism and xenophobia. Changes in the political geography of Europe led to subtle shifts in the psychology of European society. The nineties and the end of the Cold War saw the break-up of multi-national states — the USSR and the Yugoslav federation — into their constituent parts, with all of them, however tiny, laying claim to nationhood. In western Europe, the continuing construction of a greater European Union and its goal of convergence awakened concerns about national identity. Smaller nations — the Scots and Welsh and the Flemish — spotted an opportunity to assert greater independence within the wider context of Europe. The reunification of Germany, meanwhile, created the biggest and most powerful nation-state in the European Union.

In almost all cases this reaffirmation of nationhood had its ugly side. In the former Soviet Union millions of Russians emigrated from non-Russian republics, 'encouraged' by the adoption in them of anti-Russian nationality laws. In the former Yugoslavia a series of fierce nationalistic wars left the territory repartitioned along ethnic lines. Even in Scotland, devolution had a nasty streak — witness the crowds who packed cinemas to watch the film *Braveheart*, and poured into the streets shouting anti-English slogans. Everywhere people seemed to be becoming more aware of their nationality. In many places it was only a short step from this to outright racism and xenophobia.

This period of rising national sentiment coincided with crises in other parts of the world that led to influxes of refugees. Immigration into Europe peaked during the Bosnian war of 1992-95, the Kosovo conflict of 1998, and the war in Afghanistan in 2001, with a steady rise of refugees from Iraq and Turkey (mainly Kurds) throughout the decade.[1] The arrival of 3.75 million refugees seeking asylum in the European Union between 1992 and 2001 had a massive impact, which was exacerbated by government incompetence in handling them. Special refugee centres had to be built to cope with them, but many were housed together in urban, often deprived, neighbourhoods, where their presence had an unsettling effect on existing communities. Resentment grew. Asylum seekers were often branded as scroungers, even though the benefits they received were miserable, and were blamed for rising crime rates. Anti-immigrant talk in the pubs of Europe became a refrain taken up by right-wing newspapers and politicians.

In Britain they talked of being 'swamped', in Germany and Austria of '*Überfremdung*'. Little publicity was given to the reasons why so many unfortunate people had fled their homelands. The popular myth was that the vast majority of asylum seekers were 'bogus' — not escaping from persecution or indignity at all, but merely in search of a better life, at the expense of good Europeans' hard-won welfare and prosperity. The possibility that immigrants — precisely *because* they wanted to make a better life for themselves and their children in Europe — might actually contribute positively to the economy and society was given short shrift. Populist politicians promoted the idea of 'national preference' — reserving or prioritising state-provided goods and benefits (such as jobs, housing and social payments) for their own citizens, while making it as difficult as possible for immigrants to 'qualify' by obtaining citizenship.[2]

Far-right parties thrived in this climate of uncertainty. By mid-2001 they had achieved considerable successes in several countries. The Freedom Party shared power in Austria, the Vlaams Blok had marched past the 30 per cent mark at city level in Belgium, the Danish People's Party had effectively won a referendum that prevented Denmark from joining the euro, and in June Silvio Berlusconi won the Italian general election and included two extreme right politicians, Umberto Bossi and Gianfranco Fini, in his government.

Then came September 11th. The devastating co-
ordinated terrorist attacks on the World Trade Centre and
the Pentagon had an immediate impact on western
attitudes towards Muslims, who made up a large share of
those who had come to Europe in the past ten years. As the
finger of blame was pointed at Islamic extremists, there
was an upsurge of attacks, both verbal and physical, on
Muslims across Europe. The European Monitoring Centre
on Racism and Xenophobia reported a rise in
'Islamophobia', characterised by aggression against men
wearing turbans and women in Muslim *hijabs*
(headscarves), and attacks against mosques. Also, the
report said, 'A wave of anti-Semitism has unfolded in the
wake of the Middle East crisis, and the recent attacks
against Jews include posting of threatening hate mail,
vandalising of synagogues and Jewish cemeteries, and
verbal and physical assaults targeting Jews.' The British
media were particularly blamed for using negative
stereotypes of Muslims and portraying asylum seekers as
terrorists and the 'enemy within' after September 11th.[3]

In response to the attacks, western governments
adopted anti-terrorist measures — including stricter
immigration controls, an EU-wide arrest warrant, and
tough detention-without-trial laws — which were
condemned in some quarters as encroaching upon human
rights. These measures, though in theory applicable to any
suspected terrorist, were clearly aimed at Islamic funda-

mentalists. President George W. Bush's declaration of a 'war on terror', also aimed principally at Muslim countries, further cemented the notion of Islam as Enemy Number One — notwithstanding the efforts of other world leaders to draw a distinction between 'ordinary' Muslims and terrorists. The consequent wave of anti-Islamic sentiment played into the hands of the extreme right, which made immediate gains in several countries. In Britain the British National Party won seats on local councils, in Hamburg Ronald Schill's Law and Order party was swept into office, anti-immigration parties scored their best ever results in Norway, Denmark and Portugal, not to mention France, where Jean-Marie Le Pen came second in the presidential election, and Holland, where Pim Fortuyn's party rose from nowhere to become the second largest in parliament, with 26 of its 150 seats and a place in government.

But it was not just the 'refugee crisis' of the nineties or the added catalyst of September 11th that encouraged the growth of nationalism and the far right. There were also factors at play within the very political systems that were meant to defend Europe against extremism.

The European Union took great strides during the last decade of the century towards the 'ever closer union' proclaimed in its founding treaties. The single market was followed by a single currency, the euro, which became a reality in 2002. Integrationist politicians talked of a

European 'economic government' as the logical next step. Meanwhile successive treaties stripped away the right of national governments to veto EU legislation in more and more fields. A common foreign and security policy was declared a goal, and steps were taken towards a common defence strategy, with the establishment of an EU rapid reaction force, capable of carrying out military duties far beyond the geographical limits of the Union. This was decried by its critics as the embryo of a European army. There were calls for a European Constitution, and an elected president. Opposition to such federalist aspirations varied from country to country, but in most cases it was seized upon by the far right as an exploitable cause. 'Brussels' became a hate word, the symbol of lost national powers. The EU was condemned as leaving national legislatures impotent and national cultures under threat. In Austria Haider predicted a further 'swamping' of his country if the EU enlarged into central and eastern Europe, while in France Le Pen's presidential campaign in 2002 included a pledge to withdraw from the single currency and the EU itself.

Almost all far-right movements are committed to capitalism, but the advance of globalisation was another matter. Free trade brought with it a threat to national economic decision-making plus the risk of (American) cultural hegemony and multi-culturalism. So trade protectionism became another important weapon in the far right's arsenal: better to protect one's own farmers and entrepreneurs than hand control to the World Trade Organisation. The fuzzy frontiers of an increasingly globalised world, and the implied erosion of national identities, were yet another factor for the populists to exploit.

Political developments in the most stable of European countries — indeed the stability of the system itself — produced a surprising backlash. Some of the strongest far-right movements developed in countries with centrist coalition governments, where they presented themselves almost as an 'antidote' to years or decades of vapid, unadventurous rule. Proportional voting systems rarely enabled a single party to govern. Instead, coalitions — sometimes including parties with quite diverse fundamental views — became the norm. To achieve stable government, radical policies were more often than not jettisoned, and programmes followed that were merely the lowest common denominator of several parties' policies.

Consensus politics and political correctness — normally hailed as virtues — meant that important issues sometimes failed to be addressed, leaving the field wide open for the far right. The result was seen most spectacularly in the Netherlands, where Pim Fortuyn overturned decades of cosy, liberal consensus by 'breaking taboos', by lifting the veil of silence drawn over sensitive issues because they were considered beyond the pale. But it turned out that political correctness did not make awkward issues go away, it merely forced them underground, waiting for populists and demagogues to come along and unearth them. 'You have had no one in this country who could break taboos,' Haider told Austrians in a speech — meaning, until I arrived. To suggest that Islam was a 'backward culture' and that a country's borders should be shut to Muslim immigrants was deemed so unacceptable and discriminatory that the idea was never discussed in mainstream politics — until Fortuyn proclaimed it as an election pledge, and won over millions of voters. His thoughts were echoed in Italy by Berlusconi.

In Austria centrist parties did not just share political power for decades but developed an invidious *'nomenklatura'* system that divided up jobs in the state administration and public services between the social democrats and conservatives. Getting rid of this 'dual monopoly' was one of Jörg Haider's most effective promises.

Politicians like Haider and Fortuyn offered simple solutions to the alleged neglect of ordinary people's interests. They promised to stand up for 'decent ordinary folk' against 'them up there', to take on the mighty, to clean up corruption, to clear out the stables, to listen to what ordinary folk said. It was the sort of stuff that earns easy applause. Together with the right-wing press, populist politicians did not just reflect the mood emanating from public bars: they took the basest, most politically 'incorrect' views and manipulated them, giving them a veneer of respectability, and then fed them back to the crowd as election promises. As one writer put it, populist voters regarded themselves as 'a resistance movement against an empire of private greed and public hypocrisy'.[4]

✡

As outlined above, the success of the far right in recent years can largely be attributed to its exploitation of contemporary anxieties over such things as crime, immigration, unemployment, and remote, corrupt or insensitive government. It may also be argued that its roots go back much further — that modern right-wing extremism is to some extent a re-kindling of the embers of fascism, not quite doused after the Second World War. Like today's movements the fascism and Nazism of the twenties and thirties were populist, nationalist responses to the hurt and insecurity felt by the 'little man'. Hitler's Nazi party was of course obliterated in Germany's postwar denazification process, but the 'idea' (as we shall see in the chapters on Germany and Austria) was not killed off. Italy's fascists renamed and restyled themselves as the National Alliance, now led by Gianfranco Fini.

There are distinct differences, however. The early movements were in part a response to military defeat, economic depression, and the challenge of communism.

Now, the original targets of right-wing hatred have changed or disappeared. Since the fall of the Berlin Wall, communism is no longer a threat. Neither are poverty and unemployment the sources of unrest they once were: the nations of western Europe are experiencing a period of unprecedented prosperity. And even anti-Semitism is less widespread, partly because Europe's pre-war Jewish population was decimated and a Jewish state established beyond Europe; where it does occur it is often a reaction to Israeli policies in the Middle East. This has not prevented some American commentators from regarding criticism of Israel as evidence of Europe's 'reverting to type'. In fact, however, it seems an ingredient of the most successful new far-right parties that in their chase for the mainstream voter they have steered well away from anti-Semitism. Nowadays the extremists look for new scapegoats: immigrants and Muslims instead of Jews and communists.

So can or should the movements examined in this book be classified as 'fascist' or 'neo-Nazi', or is 'populist', 'authoritarian' or some other adjective more appropriate? The chapters that follow will demonstrate that the 'far right' comes in many diverse manifestations. Indeed, in some cases the term 'far right' may not seem appropriate: I shall look briefly at figures like Slobodan Miloševic, who as an ex-communist may really be 'far left', but as an ultra-nationalist, chauvinist, populist demagogue, certainly fits most of the criteria used here. I am less interested in trying to find the perfect label than to describe what the various movements and leaders are actually like — where they came from, what they stand for, and how much of a threat they are.

One thing should be made clear. None of the far-right political leaders in Europe today (apart, perhaps, from the above-mentioned and now happily deposed Milošević) is a Hitler. Though some talk of changing constitutions, they appear to have a basic respect for democracy, and do not favour a one-party system — indeed, they seem happy to exploit the possibilities afforded by democracy rather than try to overturn it. They do not advocate state control of the economy (indeed, most are fervent free-marketeers) or a massive arms build-up. They may assert the primacy of their own nations and cultures, but they are not interested in territorial conquest. For the moment the political parties, with few exceptions, exist separately from the groups of skinhead thugs who happen to support them: violence and militarism are not a part of their scheme, and none of these parties has a paramilitary wing.

What they do share with the Nazis is an essential contempt for humanity. Human beings are defined in terms of race, religion, colour, creed and national origin, with the benefits of European civilisation ring-fenced for the nationally 'pure'. The far right appeals to base instincts, searches for scapegoats for all the nation's ills, and finds fertile ground in the underprivileged classes. Its populist leaders are, however sugar-coated, preachers of hate. And their influence is spreading.

Notes

1 United Nations High Commisioner for Refugees, 31 May 2002.

2 Paul Hainsworth, 'Introduction: the Extreme Right', in *The Politics of the Extreme Right*, London: Pinter, 2000, p. 10.

3 European Monitoring Centre on Racism and Xenophobia, 'Islamophobia in the EU after September 11th 2001'.

4 Neal Ascherson, *The Observer*, 12 May 2002.

2.

Forgetful Austria

The Saviour came down to Earth in a helicopter, and the future was blue. The rotor blades spun fine powdery snow into the air. The Alpine slopes and frosted fir-trees sparkled under an azure sky, just streaked with wisps of cloud. A group of children, rosy-cheeked and warmly clad in brightly coloured ski-gear, released hundreds of blue balloons into the air. Four aeroplanes of the 'Team 2000' stunt squadron staged a fly-past. Men in Lederhosen clasped blue bottles of Jörg beer, and cauldrons of hearty potato soup and blood sausage were stirred over open fires. There was singing and dancing, and the Golob folk music band played oompah-music on the instruments they had hauled some 2,000 feet up the mountainside for the occasion.

It was Jörg Haider's fiftieth birthday, and he and thousands of his supporters had taken over Mount Gerlitzen in the Carinthian Alps to celebrate. Eventually Haider departed, flanked by the province's best skiers, and descended the mountain to the sound of 'Iron Man', a rock song composed in his honour, with the words: 'We are strong, we are young, we are the iron man.' The celebrations had, in the words of Haider's biographer, 'fascistic overtones... it's all about manipulation of the masses around the figure of one man.'[1]

But the adoring crowds were not just celebrating his birthday. Jörg Haider was just days away from gaining the power he had dreamt of all his adult life — seats for his radical right-wing Freedom Party in Austria's federal government. It was Saturday 30 January 2000, and for four months since the general election in October, when the Freedom Party had come second with 27.2 per cent of the vote, coalition talks had been going on between the Social Democrats (33.4 per cent) led by Chancellor Viktor Klima, and the conservative Austrian People's Party of Wolfgang Schüssel, the dapper bow-tied foreign minister in the outgoing administration (in third place with 26.9 per cent). Schüssel had vowed not to join a coalition if he was forced into third place, while Klima — in line with the Social Democrats' policy of *Ausgrenzung*, or shunning, of the extreme right — was determined not to go into partnership with Haider. So there was stalemate, until Klima finally gave up his efforts to form a government, and President Thomas Klestil invited the centre-right Schüssel and far-right Haider to open coalition talks — while wringing his hands and assuring the world, in an extraordinary admission of how precarious he felt the situation was, that democracy and pluralism were still alive in Austria.

Though Haider by now was leading national opinion polls, he could not shake off the impression given by remarks scattered over the past decade or so that he was a Nazi sympathiser: he had praised Hitler's employment policies and spoken warmly of some Waffen SS veterans. In an interview with me the day after the election he said he now regretted some of those remarks. 'I think you have to regret them,' he said, 'because it's difficult to explain a complex historical process in a few words.' Regarding his comment on the Nazis' employment policies, he said: 'It was only one sentence in a statement in the parliament, and my political opponents picked one sentence up and turned it into a campaign against me.' As for his meeting with SS veterans, 'I met them at a meeting. I couldn't know who was among the audience. I think this is the risk for a politician during all meetings.'

These excuses, as we shall see, were far from the truth, and cut little ice abroad. The French president Jacques Chirac telephoned President Klestil to express his misgivings at the prospect of Haider's party entering government. Other European leaders, including the Belgian and Portuguese prime ministers, also expressed their concern, while the Israeli leader Ehud Barak called for a 'united international front' to block the Freedom Party.

At his mountainside birthday party, surrounded by his usual entourage of muscular, sun-tanned young men, Haider's response was typically undiplomatic. President Chirac, he said, didn't know what he was talking about, and anyway — he felt obliged to add — 'in recent years he's done just about everything wrong that it's possible to do'. As for the Belgian government, they'd do better to deal with their paedophiles and corruption scandals instead of lecturing Austrians.

With the European Union threatening to freeze diplomatic contacts with Austria if the planned coalition went ahead, Haider moved to quell fears over his past remarks about the Nazi period. He said his voters included no Nazi sympathisers and described Hitler's crimes as the worst of the twentieth century, adding that no one who wished to serve in government could identify with them. People should accept his apology for having made the remarks.

Haider had made clear that he himself would not become a minister in the new government: he intended to remain governor of his native province, Carinthia. But as leader of the Freedom Party he was intimately involved in drawing up the new government's programme, together with Wolfgang Schüssel, and it was he who took centre stage under the gilt cornices and chandeliers of the Hofburg palace on 3 February to sign a solemn pledge to uphold the principles of European democracy. This was a condition set by the heavy-hearted President Klestil, still hoping to avert EU sanctions. In a magazine interview published that day he made clear his deep unease about what he was doing. He said the Freedom Party leaders used language that [theoretically] disqualified them from political office. As for Wolfgang Schüssel, his manoeuvrings to become chancellor gave the president gooseflesh.[2]

Nonetheless, the Freedom Party took six of the twelve ministerial posts, including that of vice-chancellor. But in a sign that Klestil really did feel he was supping with the devil, he rejected two candidates nominated by Haider because of their murky past.

Meanwhile, thousands of protesters marched through the streets and packed the enormous Heldenplatz, helpfully reminding foreign journalists that this was where Hitler had addressed the Austrian people from a balcony after he annexed Austria in 1938. While Klestil, Schüssel and Haider put the finishing touches to their documents inside the Hofburg, the crowd outside grew angrier, beating drums, blowing whistles and throwing paint, eggs and stones at riot police. Peaceful, democratic Austria had never seen anything like it. A country universally admired for its moderation, its Scandinavian-style welfare state, its neutrality and its social peace, now seemed on the brink of catastrophe.

The European Union carried out its threat to impose diplomatic sanctions against one of its own members, unheard of in the Union's history. The Portuguese prime minister, Antonio Guterres, justifying the move, said: 'If a party which has expressed xenophobic views, and which does not abide by the essential values of the European family, comes to power, naturally we won't be able to continue the same relations as in the past, however much we regret it. Nothing will be as before.' It meant that Freedom Party ministers, such as the youthful Karl-Heinz Grasser, the finance minister, were henceforth shunned by their fellows. At the Lisbon summit of EU prime ministers in March, no traditional 'family photo' was taken, as Schüssel's fourteen colleagues desperately found excuses to ignore him. Austrian ambassadors were received only 'at a technical level', with political discussions banned.

The question that nagged everyone was this: was the EU over-reacting? Was Haider as bad as he seemed? And with 27 per cent of voters behind him, what did this say about the Austrian people? Was there a dark side to this nation that was only now coming to the surface? Was Haiderism merely a response to contemporary troubles, or did it grow out of Austria's history?

✳

The trouble with Austria was that ever since the War it had consistently tried to bury its past. Unlike the Germans, who were guilt-ridden about the Nazi period and their complicity in the Holocaust and the other monstrous crimes committed under Hitler, the Austrians had never truly faced up to the part they played during that period. After the War a fiction was constructed that Austria had been Hitler's 'first victim' — invaded and annexed in 1938.

The phrase even found its way into the State Treaty of 1955 which established Austria as a neutral state after ten years of post-war occupation by the four victorious powers — Britain, France, the USA and the Soviet Union. Legitimacy was thus given to the Austrians' self-delusion that they bore no responsibility for the outrages of the Third Reich — that atonement for Nazi sins and soul-searching about how to prevent a recurrence were things for Germans to occupy themselves with, not Austrians.

In fact, as the rest of the world knew, the Nazis had been met with celebration, not resistance, in Austria. Hitler received a hero's welcome in Vienna. Many Austrians had collaborated with the regime, signing up to

the Nazi Party with alacrity, working as 'willing execu-
tioners'. Recruitment to the army and the elite SS was
easy. There was widespread support for a 'strong hand' to
sort out the economic and political chaos of the thirties.
Anschluss — incorporation into a greater Germany —
matched the pan-German aspirations of many Austrians,
and the military discipline and anti-Semitism preached by
Hitler found a strong resonance here. The confiscation of
Jewish property was hugely popular, especially in Vienna,
where anti-Semitism had deep roots. Later, the indefatigable Nazi-hunter, Simon Wiesenthal, tried to alert the
country's new leaders to his findings that Austria's civil
service and judiciary were still peppered with former
Nazis, that denazification had been shockingly
inadequate, and that there was 'extensive proof that
Austrians were responsible for the deaths of three million
Jews (out of the estimated six million killed)' — yet there
had been far fewer war crimes trials in Austria than in
Germany.[3]

When the War was over, though, it was extremely
convenient for Austria's 536,000 former Nazi party
members (including Jörg Haider's parents) to paint
themselves as victims rather than collaborators. The myth
made it easy for ex-Nazis to continue to be involved in
public life — indeed, a positive effort was made to
reintegrate them, rather than leaving a large group of
potentially dangerous or subversive right-wingers outside

the political system. Former Nazis were excluded from voting in the first general election in 1945, but were allowed to participate in the next one, in 1949, after denaz-ification laws passed in 1946 and 1947 were naïvely believed to have eliminated their influence from public life. In fact, because Austrians were given to believe they bore no trace of war guilt, and because there was no suggestion that they had been involved in persecution and consequently owed restitution to their victims, there was little exploration of what had really happened. Western countries were in any case already more interested in fighting the new communist foe than in digging over Austria's unsavoury past or in searching for Nazis there. Indeed, while in Germany wrestling with the Nazi past became an obsession, in Austria it was almost taboo.

The result was an atmosphere of complacency, in which Nazi ideas did not merely lie dormant, but thrived. The old Nazi party was banned, of course, but its followers found scope for their sentiments in right-wing student societies or *Burschenschaften*, which combined militaristic sports with Nazi-style discipline and German nationalist politics. Archive film from the sixties shows a boyish Jörg Haider at a meeting of one of these clubs, with a Monkees hair-do, a wide red tie and plump, ruddy cheeks. He sits at a long table, flanked by young men in uniforms, sashes and peaked caps, listening to political speeches and mouthing along with patriotic songs. Out of these associations grew neo-Nazi political parties — including, in 1956, the Freedom Party, led by a former SS officer, Anton Reinthaller. In elections it scored only around 5 per cent, and came to be regarded as sufficiently benign, liberal even, to be admitted to the Liberal International in 1979 and to be included in a coalition government with the Socialists in 1983. But that was all to change.

Two events in the mid-eighties conspired to change the face of Austrian politics and propel Haider to prominence. For forty years the myth about Austria as Hitler's 'first victim' had scarcely been challenged. Former Nazis and neo-Nazis lived comfortably in the knowledge that their past lives were forgotten and forgiven. They had been subsumed into 'mainstream' politics. Then, in 1985, Austria's defence minister, Friedhelm Frischenschläger — the son of a Nazi, but on the democratic wing of the Freedom Party — committed a faux pas which dramatically exposed the lie. At an airfield near Graz he welcomed home, with a fateful handshake that shocked liberals at home and abroad, a convicted Nazi war criminal, SS Major Walter Reder, who had had his life sentence in an Italian jail, for his role in the mass murder of Italian civilians during the War, commuted, and was returning to Austria. Frischenschläger was supported by Jörg Haider, who was by now leader of the Freedom Party in the southern province of Carinthia and eager to shift his party away from its centrist liberalism: in an early example of the kind of statements that would come to haunt him, he described Reder not as a war criminal but as 'a soldier like hundreds of thousands of others, who fulfilled his duty as required by his oath'.[4] But elsewhere the handshake caused a furore. The eyes of a world beguiled by Austria's image as a contented land of Strauss waltzes and *The Sound of Music* were suddenly opened. Under the carpet of edelweiss, a dark, unexplored history still lurked.

The following year that history was brought even more sharply into focus when Kurt Waldheim, who had served two terms as Secretary General of the United Nations, stood as a candidate for Austrian president and found himself at the centre of a storm over his wartime record. Unearthed documents showed him to have been an interpreter and intelligence officer for a German army unit in the Balkans which, among other things, had deported most of the Jewish population of Thessaloniki in Greece to Nazi death camps in 1943 — at a time when Waldheim had claimed he was studying law at Vienna University. The World Jewish Congress discovered documents proving he had been a member of the Nazi Youth League, and labelled him a liar. Waldheim denied any connection with wartime atrocities. But abroad his reputation plummeted, and the run-up to the presidential election was marred by a daily barrage of accusations. Once again, the spotlight was thrown on that part of Austria's past which had been swept under the carpet. And once again the reaction at home was to rally round the 'victim': Waldheim was elected to a six-year term with almost 54 per cent of the vote. (The EU might usefully have borne that in mind when it imposed sanctions over the Haider affair in 2000.)

The Times wrote at the end of Waldheim's term: 'The Waldheim scandal exposed an unpleasant side of the country; its anti-Semitic undertones and a tendency to indulge in collective amnesia. It resulted not in a more exacting examination of the past, but in its citizens closing ranks resentfully against the rest of the world. The Third Reich continues to sit like an undigested lump in the body politic.'[5]

One man was ready to exploit the sense of unease and national humiliation caused by the Reder handshake and the Waldheim debacle. At the Freedom Party's congress in Innsbruck later in 1986, Jörg Haider gathered extreme-right grass roots support to mount a stunning putsch against the party's moderate leadership. He was over-whelmingly elected as the new leader — and his fans roared 'Sieg heil!' in raucous celebration. In view of its lurch to the right, the Social Democrats immediately ended their coalition with the Freedom Party and vowed to exclude it henceforth from high public office. But under Haider it was to go from strength to strength.

✡

Haider played on the Austrians' sense of slight. There were hundreds of thousands of Waldheims out there, who either denied their part in the Nazi system, or insisted they had 'only been doing their duty', or believed there was nothing wrong with it all. Haider set out to make them feel good again, to restore their 'self-respect'. Many of his infamous remarks can be seen in this light.

In his book, *The Freedom I mean*, he wrote: 'At any rate an end has to be put to the constant criminalisation of our own history, as though the life of the war generation was nothing but a rogues' gallery.'[6] Asked by a newspaper which historical figures he loathed the most, Haider replied, not Hitler or any of his henchmen, but 'Churchill and Stalin'.[7]

One pro-Nazi remark cost him his first high-profile job. In 1989 the Freedom Party came second in elections in Haider's home province of Carinthia. Haider became *Landeshauptmann* or governor, as part of a coalition deal with the third-placed centre-right People's Party, designed to keep the Social Democrats out of power. Two years later, in the course of a heated debate on the economy, he blurted out: 'In the Third Reich they had a proper [*ordentliche*] employment policy, which is something your government in Vienna can't manage.'[8] The People's Party promptly terminated the coalition, and Haider was out of office.

Most notoriously, in September 1995 he addressed a reunion in Krumpendorf, Carinthia, of Waffen-SS veterans

— men from the most brutal of Nazi units, fanatical racists who served as Hitler's personal bodyguard, administered the concentration camps, and carried out mass executions. (The SS was declared a criminal organisation by the Nuremberg Tribunal in 1946.) What Haider said contained not just words of comfort for old men, to reassure them their lives had not been in vain: he went out of his way to praise the *principles* they had fought for. 'And that is the reason ultimately why I believe one must have a counter-balance, otherwise we really would be living in a world of chaos, and that is not what you fought for and risked your lives for. You did that so that later generations and young people would have a future in a community still governed by the principles of order, justice and decency. [...] There is no argument [against Waffen-SS reunions] other than irritation that there are still people of character in this world who have stood up for their beliefs against all the odds and have remained true to their convictions to this day.'[9]

Did Haider really have to go that far? This, after all, was in 1995, when he had already turned the Freedom Party into a powerful force that was heading for even greater victories. One might have expected him to be more circumspect. The Krumpendorf speech, true, was filmed secretly — perhaps he did not expect what appear to be his real views to gain a wider audience. But it did him no harm. The Freedom Party's share of the vote grew further, evidence that by reassessing Austria's Nazi past in a positive way (not at all what was envisaged by 'denazification') he had struck a chord among many in the older generation. This was sheer populism, and it worked.

Haider's leadership had a dramatic effect on the fortunes of the Freedom Party, which accounted for less than 5 per cent of the vote in 1986 when he took control of it. In the 1990 federal election the party took 15 per cent, in 1994 more than 24 per cent, and in the 1996 European Parliament elections 28 per cent, while at provincial level it did even better, culminating in Haider's record 43 per cent in Carinthia in March 1999 — allowing him to reclaim the governorship he had lost eight years earlier, this time with no need to rely on coalition partners.

His success was not just down to his exploitation of the national preference for amnesia about the Third Reich. If that were all he stood for, his popularity might not have extended much beyond the dwindling numbers of Nazi-era pensioners. There were other ills in modern Austrian society that he latched on to and turned into popular political causes — not least the discredited *Proporz* system, under which the two mainstream political parties, the Social Democrats and the People's Party, divided all important jobs in the public and private sector (and indeed many less important ones) between their supporters, according to the proportion of votes each received at elections.

The system had been introduced by the victorious powers after the war as a means of preventing extremists, particularly ex-Nazis, from holding office in the civil service, and of ensuring stability by weighting appointments in favour of the centrist parties. But the system had atrophied into a much-despised network of officially approved cronyism. It was widely perceived to have led to corruption and privilege. Ironically it was one of the few parts of Austria's denazification process that had been pursued with rigour — and yet it lingered long after most former Nazis were well past retirement age and no longer in line for public service positions anyway. Now it was seen as principally the means by which the Establishment kept itself in power, handing out 'jobs for the boys'. This was a prime target for Haider, who set himself up as the friend of the 'little man' and promised to fight back on his behalf against the bureaucracy, the Establishment, and the corrupt levers of power.

The system had no parallel in western Europe: it was closer to the *nomenklatura* system in the Soviet bloc, whereby the Communist Party extended its control throughout society by vetting and controlling all public appointments. Austria's *Proporz* system differed from this only in the sense that two parties rather than one handed out the jobs. The result was truly bizarre, as one newspaper correspondent described: 'There are two automobile clubs, one for conservative Austrians and the other for those with social democrat inclinations. Many sports clubs tend to function in the same way. Schools have Red or Black leanings — the head will be a card-carrying member. Hospitals, libraries, museums and universities are all bricks in the party state. Above a certain level, you cannot rise without the party book.'[10] The Freedom Party was not a member of this club, so Haider vowed: 'We shall do away with the party state.'

A picture emerges, then, of a man who not only demonstrates some sort of continuity with the Nazi past — by being at the very least ambivalent about it and by pandering to those still attached to it — but has also seized upon an undoubted fault in the post-war system and vowed to eradicate it. And there is another facet to Haider: his opportunism. Since taking over the Freedom Party he has jumped on — and off — several bandwagons that offered vote-winning opportunities.

One of those opportunities came with the fall of the Berlin Wall and the collapse of communism in eastern Europe in 1989. In the summer of that year the Hungarian government literally pulled down the Iron Curtain by removing the barbed-wire fencing along its border with Austria. It wasn't just Hungarians who took the chance to come west, but other nationalities, including East Germans, who streamed across in their little Trabant cars. The sight of people escaping from communism — or merely coming across to sniff the air — delighted most in the West, but in Austria it sent shivers down many spines: as the frontline country there were fears that it could be inundated with poor foreigners seeking not just freedom but work and benefits — at a time when Austrians themselves were worrying about losing their jobs. The collapse of Yugoslavia and the wars in Croatia and Bosnia did indeed bring an influx of immigrants, mostly heading for the big cities like Vienna. Haider spotted the insecurities and resentments felt particularly among the city's working classes, and launched the first of his crusades against immigration. He did not need to wait until large numbers started coming: the *fear* of a flood was enough to stoke up xenophobia. He warned of '*Überfremdung*' — an emotive word that conjures up images of a land swamped by foreigners. (The word, once used by Hitler's propaganda minister, Joseph Goebbels, had Nazi connotations.) In the Vienna city elections in November 1991 the Freedom Party's slogan was 'Vienna for the Viennese'; it secured them 22.5 per cent of the vote — twice their previous tally.

Fortified by this success, Haider started a campaign for an end to immigration altogether. A national petition promoted by the Freedom Party in 1993 gathered 'only' 416,000 signatures — far fewer than the million Haider had called for. Statistically it was a failure, but it was enough to scare the governing right-left coalition, which responded by imposing severe immigration restrictions anyway. (In much the same way, most EU countries tightened their rules on asylum seekers and immigration in 2002, following more right-wing extremist successes around Europe.)

After the (relative) failure of his petition, Haider moved rapidly to his next subject — Austria's application to join the European Union. Negotiations for entry began in 1993, with the focus on squaring Austria's neutrality with its integration into a bloc moving steadily towards a common foreign and security policy. Haider zig-zagged. Initially he had supported Austrian membership as a means of drawing his country closer to Germany, but during the campaign he opposed it, on the grounds that Vienna would cede sovereignty to Brussels. As for the question of neutrality, Haider — ever contrary — called for Austria to join NATO. When a referendum on EU membership in June 1994 showed two-thirds of Austrians to be in favour, however, Haider dropped that issue and went on to campaign instead against membership of the single currency and the enlargement of the EU. When the government nonetheless decided to take Austria into the euro-zone, Haider backed down, and by the end of the decade — in words, at least — he appeared to be reconciling himself to the fact that neighbouring countries like Hungary, the Czech Republic, Slovakia and Slovenia would soon be joining the European Union.

The prospect of workers from these countries having ready access to Austrian jobs, however, remained a card he would play to the full. This time he dressed up his xenophobia as concern for Austrian workers, and launched a fresh anti-immigration campaign. Freedom Party posters in the 1999 election campaign called for 'An end to *Über-fremdung*' and 'An end to asylum abuse'. 'Because of the possibility of naturalisation after six years, and because of [EU] expansion to the East,' Haider said, 'we are threatened by a further flood of foreigners. I suspect the federal government wants to create a new electorate for itself because it can no longer be sure of the old one.'[11]

A Freedom Party election broadcast in Vienna in 1999 contained the following assertions:

'Did you know ... that our Vienna children are already being force-fed Turkish and Serbo-Croat texts in their German reading books? ... that under the Social Democrats in Vienna black African asylum seekers with designer suits and state-of-the-art mobile phones can go about their drugs-dealing business with impunity? ... that the Social Democrats in Vienna grant Austrian citizenship, usually without proper consideration, to 9,300 foreigners a year, and that they thereby acquire the right to vote and have access to municipal housing?'

One of Haider's closest lieutenants, Thomas Prinzhorn, a Harvard-educated economist who was to have become finance minister in the right-wing coalition formed in 2000, made the following startling claim: 'The foreigners receive free hormone treatment from the social welfare office to increase their fertility. Austrians are only rarely offered this.' The following day Prinzhorn said he 'regretted' his words had been taken in a xenophobic way: he had not 'meant it like that'. But he added: 'It is a fact that they have free access, I've checked that out.' Prinzhorn was one of the Freedom Party candidates for a ministerial post whom President Klestil rejected.

Haider made it clear from the outset that he himself would not serve in the federal government formed in February 2000. When his party went into coalition with Chancellor Wolfgang Schüssel he even stepped down from the leadership of the Freedom Party, in favour of Susanne Riess-Passer, who became deputy chancellor. Most observers suspected that he wanted to keep his copybook clean if the Freedom Party's sortie into government at national level failed: his eyes were firmly on the chancellorship next time round. He claimed he wanted to make clear that his cronies in the government were not his puppets, but no one doubted — indeed Riess-Passer confirmed it — that he remained firmly in charge of Freedom Party policy-making, even if formally he was no more than governor of Carinthia.

*

Carinthia and its capital, Klagenfurt, are Haider's adopted home and power-base. He was born in Bad Goisern, in Upper Austria, in 1950. His father, a shoemaker, and his mother, a teacher, joined the Nazi Party in 1929 when it was illegal, nine years before Hitler annexed Austria. Their plight after the war helped to mould his political character. Their house in Bad Goisern was in ruins, and as a former Nazi his mother was forbidden to teach. They claimed to have known nothing about the concentration camps, and felt unjustly persecuted. But other members of Haider's family profited from Hitler's programme of 'Aryanisation', under which Jewish property was confiscated and sold at bargain prices to Germans. Haider inherited a huge estate from his great uncle, William Webhofer, who bought it in 1939 from its Jewish owner for about a tenth of its real value.

His early political ideas were formed under the influence of his parents and two right-wing clubs which he joined — the Austrian Sports Union, where he learned to fence but also absorbed its leaders' neo-fascist views, and a fraternity (*Burschenschaft*) of uniformed students led by former Nazis who supervised everything from the beer-drinking to the debating club. At the age of 16 he won a debating contest on the theme: 'Are we Austrians Germans?' (It was a topic that preoccupied him: as late as 1988, using orthodox Nazi vocabulary, he described the Austrian nation as an 'ideological miscarriage', though later he would abandon his German-nationalist views in favour of Austrian nationalism.) His fencing also progressed well. According to a friend, he used to practise on a straw doll to which was pinned the name of the Nazi-hunter Simon Wiesenthal.[12]

He moved to Carinthia at the age of 26 to become secretary of the province's branch of the Freedom Party. The region borders Slovenia (which was then part of Yugoslavia), and the local party was traditionally right-wing, directing its xenophobia in particular at its small Slovene minority. The party made common cause with a chauvinist pan-Germanic organisation known as the *Kärntner Heimatdienst* (Carinthian Homeland Service) which campaigned against bilingual traffic signs and for the abolition of bilingual primary education. From 1989 to 1991 Haider enjoyed his first brief spell as governor, before being turfed out after his praise for Hitler's employment policies. When he was re-elected in April 1999 he introduced a number of populist 'Austrians first' policies. He reduced rents and energy prices in Carinthia and began introducing *Kindergeld* or 'children's money' — a 6,000 Schillings (€436/£274) per month benefit for Austrian children. He wanted to introduce it throughout the country, while reducing income tax to a flat rate of 23 per cent — populist proposals dismissed by his opponents as unrealistic. (The federal government did in fact introduce *Kindergeld* throughout the country in 2002.)

Apart from tapping into popular grievances, much of Haider's success stemmed from his personality. He is permanently tanned and full of energy, addresses crowds with great animation, and undoubtedly has charisma. Hans-Peter Martin, a member of the European parliament, says he 'behaves and is accepted like a very attractive ski-school teacher'. But since he took over the Freedom Party in 1986 he has also rigorously moulded it in his own image, enforcing strict discipline and edging out all rivals.

One observer described how Haider appealed to the inferiority complex in the Austrian mentality: 'Always the losers, always done down — abandoned to the Prussians by Maria Theresa, squashed politically by Metternich, totally humiliated in 1866 at the Battle of Königgrätz, then threatened by the Slavs, betrayed by the Hungarians, dominated by the Germans and finally seduced by them into disaster (and later almost always even beaten by them at football), skilled at forgetting their own monstrous crimes, and now threatened by foreigners snatching at their housing, jobs and welfare benefits... what a wonderful, awful world! Who can help? For more than ten years now the disenfranchised have had a hero, the Robin Hood of the Bärental [Carinthia]: Jörg Haider.'[13] The writer described Haider as 'the demagogue, who knows his people and their neuroses, politicises their complaints — their carping and grumbling and envy — and uses this to attack the real injustice of the system, of the

Establishment parties, the boardrooms, the unions, the fat cats, the foreigners and the alarmists abroad.'

One of Haider's ex-colleagues, the party's former general secretary, Heide Schmidt, put it more brutally as she stomped out of the Freedom Party in 1993 to set up a new, truly Liberal party: Haider, she said, was a *Menschenverächter* — a 'despiser of mankind'.

✻

Vienna was once one of Europe's great Jewish cities. Some 200,000 Jews lived here until the Nazis almost wiped them out. Now only a small number remain, but they say anti-Semitism has never really gone away. Jörg Haider has been careful not to make overtly anti-Jewish statements, but many Vienna Jews are appalled by his tendency to equate the suffering of the Germans (the bombing of Dresden, the expulsion of Germans from the Sudetenland and Silesia) with that of the Jews.

I went to see Leon Zelman, head of the Jewish Welcome Service, which helps to connect visiting or returning Jews to their Viennese heritage. A bustling, slightly grumpy 72-year-old, he met me on the pavement and guided me at top speed along Kafkaesque stairways and corridors crammed with piled-up documents and books to his office, where he hammered on the door and barked at his secretary for taking too long to open it — and then looked sheepishly contrite about his behaviour. You could forgive a little grumpiness, though, in a man who spent his teenage years in Auschwitz. He presented me with a copy of his book, *After Survival*, which contains stomach-churning memories of what he witnessed as a youth.

What he wanted to talk about, however, wasn't the death camps, but Vienna — his adopted home city. He chose to come here when he was freed after the War, and said he intentionally shut his eyes to its defects — especially the anti-Semitism which, he said, 'quietly permeated the entire society'. Was this relevant, I wondered, to Haider's growing popularity? After all, he was not on record as ever having made any anti-Jewish remark.

'That's true,' said Zelman. 'It's not the anti-Semitism that worries me. It's the atmosphere.' He described how he had sat in his room above St Stephen's Square and watched — and listened — to a huge Haider rally shortly before the October 1999 election. The way Haider manipulated the crowd, the way they cheered, the whipping up of hatred and intolerance — that was what scared him, and reminded him of Nazi rallies he had witnessed as a boy. 'It reminded me how open people are to big ideas, how easy it is make them shout "Bravo! Bravo!"' He said he had wept at the memory.

There were other centres of opposition to Haider too. The Vienna national theatre, the Burgtheater, became a focus for protests by liberal intellectuals. The Archbishop of Vienna called a news conference to declare that Austria faced its greatest crisis since the Second World War, with society riven through the middle, and the whole country declared beyond the pale in Europe. Left-wingers staged a protest march every Thursday evening from the moment the Freedom Party entered government.

And yet, once in power, the Freedom Party gained credibility and respectability. The declaration which Haider signed, as a condition for joining the coalition, not only bound the party to respect the principles of European democracy, but explicitly committed the government (and therefore the Freedom Party) to work 'for an Austria in which xenophobia, anti-Semitism and racism have no place'. The declaration contained the following paragraph, which went further than anything before to correct the impression that Austria had merely been a victim of Hitler.

Austria accepts her responsibility arising out of the tragic history of the 20th century and the horrendous crimes of the National Socialist regime. Our country is facing up to the light and dark sides of its past and to the deeds of all Austrians, good and evil, as its responsibility. Nationalism, dictatorship and intolerance brought war, xenophobia, bondage, racism and mass murder. The singularity of the crimes of the Holocaust which are without precedent in history are an exhortation to permanent alertness against all forms of dictatorship and totalitarianism.

The six Freedom Party ministers — including those for the key posts of justice, defence and finance — were careful not to put a foot wrong. The new government moved swiftly to address its critics' fears, indeed it tended to over-compensate. Where the previous moderate left-right coalition, for example, had dragged its feet for years over compensation for Nazi victims, the Schüssel government immediately appointed a special officer, a former president of the Austrian national bank, to deal with claims by former slave labourers. In July 2000 the government set up a fund of 6 billion Schillings (€436m/£274m) to be shared among the 150,000 Jewish and other slave labourers still alive.

By September a committee of 'Wise Men' appointed by the EU to assess the Freedom Party's impact on government had to concede that 'the Austrian government has not failed in its commitment to uphold European common values'. The sanctions imposed by Austria's fourteen EU partners had, in effect, backfired, making the Freedom Party more popular than ever and fuelling Austrians' resentment over the meddling and prejudice of outsiders. 'The measures have already generated nationalist sentiments in Austria, above all because they have sometimes been wrongly interpreted as sanctions against the Austrian people.' Only one Freedom Party minister, the minister of justice Dieter Böhmdorfer was singled out for criticism — for threatening legal action against political opponents if they criticised the government. The Wise Men recommended that the sanctions be lifted, while cautioning: 'The Freedom Party can be qualified as a right-wing populist party with extremist characteristics and its evolution is uncertain.'

So had Haider changed or not? He certainly found it difficult to stop himself making controversial statements, even while staying 'in the background' in Carinthia while his cronies worked in the government. In February 2001 he accused Ariel Muzicant, the head of Austria's Jewish community, of 'unclean business practices' and drew raucous laughter at a beer-hall gathering of Freedom Party members by making fun of Muzicant's first name (the same as a brand of washing powder): 'How can a man with such a name have such dirt on his hands?' Chancellor Schüssel tried to dismiss the joke as 'carnivalesque ribaldry', but Muzicant and the Jewish community were outraged. Haider withdrew the remarks under threat of legal action.

His party resorted again to anti-immigrant slogans in the March 2001 city elections in Vienna. It won only 21 per cent, however — 7 points less than in the previous election. It seemed that the Freedom Party — now regarded as a compliant coalition partner at national level, and lacking Haider's high-profile leadership — was losing support.

It may not be accidental that the Freedom Party's failing fortunes coincided with a worrying upsurge in neo-Nazi activity — something virtually unheard of in Austria until then. The lack of skinhead violence, which is much more common in Germany, had been attributed in part to the existence of the Freedom Party in the mainstream of Austrian politics, which meant far-right sympathisers did not feel marginalised. But in April 2002 there was a skinhead demonstration in the Heldenplatz, organised by the neo-Nazi *Kameradschaft Germania* group and attended by a former Freedom Party politician. Afterwards some of the skinheads marched through the centre of Vienna shouting 'Sieg Heil!' A few weeks later, on 8 May, far-right fraternities demonstrated at the Hofburg to commemorate the anniversary of Nazi Germany's capitulation. The main speaker was the Freedom Party's ombudsman.

Jörg Haider himself appeared to be biding his time. He still courted controversy — by visiting Saddam Hussein in Iraq, for example — but no one imagined that he regarded his career at national level to be over. Indeed, he appeared to have greater aspirations, too. In 2002, following the success of the French far-right leader, Jean-Marie Le Pen, in the presidential elections, Haider launched the idea of a pan-European far-right platform. He told the Italian newspaper *Corriere della Sera* that the forthcoming European parliament elections in 2004 could be the moment to launch 'a common platform for all populist parties in Europe' as an antidote to the 'Europe of bureaucrats'.[14] Haider's political antennae again sensed the mood: he singled out crime, immigration, traditional family values and corruption as the chief worries in society, and said people all over Europe were rebelling because of the lack of response to these issues by their governments. 'A gap has developed between the people and the political Establishment.' Once again, the outsider was setting himself up as the real or only voice of opposition — the people's tribune, raging against the machine.

In the late summer of 2002 a natural disaster handed him an unexpected opportunity to hasten his comeback at national level, but for once his political judgment seemed to fail him. Disastrous floods had swept across the country, causing great damage. The government — including Haider's party colleagues, deputy chancellor Riess-Passer and finance minister Karl-Heinz Grasser, who had done much to soften the Freedom Party's extreme image — agreed as a result to postpone planned tax cuts, in order to pay for the huge repairs bill. This cut across one of the Freedom Party's prime election promises, and Haider decided to precipitate a crisis by condemning the decision and forcing his colleagues in government to resign. That gave Chancellor Schüssel no option but to pull out of the coalition and call snap elections for November. Haider was expected to be re-elected national party leader, but many members were unhappy about his humiliation of the popular Riess-Passer, and he decided not to put himself forward, saying he was stepping back altogether from national politics. The Freedom Party was left in disarray. It was unclear whether, without Haider, it would be able to stage a comeback — and unclear, too, whether Haider, who had resigned or threatened resignation several times before, really meant it this time.

Notes

1 *Sunday Telegraph*, 30 January 2000. See also Christa Zöchling, *Haider: eine Karriere*, Munich: Econ Taschenbuch Verlag, 2000.

2 *News*, 3 February 2000.

3 Quoted in Hella Pick, *Guilty Victim*, London: I.B.Tauris, 2000.

4 *Kärntner Nachrichten*, 14 February 1985.

5 *The Times*, 25 April 1992, cited in Pick, *op. cit.*, p.150.

6 J. Haider, *Die Freiheit, die ich meine*, Frankfurt/M., Berlin, 1993, p. 116.

7 *Kleine Zeitung*, 29 January 1989.

8 *Protokoll der Sitzung des Kärntner Landtages*, 13 June 1991.

[9] Transcript provided by the Dokumentationsarchiv des Österreichischen Widerstandes.

[10] Imre Karacs in *The Independent*, 4 February 2000.

[11] *Die Presse*, 10 July 1998.

[12] *The Guardian*, 2 February 2000.

[13] Werner A. Perger in *Die Zeit*, 8/2000.

[14] *The Guardian*, 31 May 2002.

3.

Vigilant Germany

In Germany, unlike Austria, the far right's influence is felt more in the streets than at the ballot-boxes. Several extremist parties exist, but their memberships and share of the vote at elections has stagnated or dwindled over the past decade. (The success of the anti-immigration politician, Ronald Schill, in Hamburg in 2001 was the one notable exception, and even that was not repeated in national elections the following year.) But the incidence of skinhead violence and even murder by racist individuals or groups has grown. The authorities try to keep a precise tally of known right-wing extremists, and noted that in 2001 their numbers had fallen from 50,900 the previous year to 49,700, while the number of those 'prepared to use violence' rose from 9,700 to 10,400. Even more alarming, more than seven hundred violent crimes were committed that year by neo-Nazis and skinheads, most of them directed against foreigners and a small number against Jews and left-wingers.[1] In the ten years after German reunification in 1990 — a decade that saw right-wing violence soar — as many as 32 people (unofficially 100) were killed by right-wing extremists.[2] It is a disturbing problem, and a major political issue in a country still haunted by its past. An entire department of the Federal Office for the Protection of the Constitution exists to analyse and counter the phenomenon, with similar departments in each of the sixteen states.

If the Austrians tended to shy away from discussion of the Nazi past for most of the post-War years, the Germans by contrast were obsessed with it. One only needs to look at the covers of news magazines such as *Der Spiegel* or *Stern* over the past decades to see the frequency with which editors resorted to pictures of Hitler or concentration camps, and headline words such as 'the past' or 'guilt'. There was an acute awareness — and still is — of the utter calamity wrought upon Europe by Germany under National Socialism. The figure of 6,000,000 Jews killed in the Holocaust clangs like a bell in the national psyche. Thinkers, writers, journalists have wrestled with the question 'Why did it happen?' There were two distinct reasons for this probing. One, to search into the souls of the generation that carried out these atrocities, to analyse what went wrong, to dissect the German mentality and try to discover if there was something genetically wrong with it, or whether the monstrous aberration of the thirties was the equivalent of a national mental breakdown. The second reason is to draw lessons, and prevent it from happening again.

Politically, a new generation came to power in Germany with the election of Chancellor Gerhard Schröder in 1998. His government comprised people whose views were formed in the student protests of 1968 rather than the Hitler Youth or the years of War. In the sixties they too had agonised over the Germans' guilt — but specifically over the guilt of their parents. They themselves felt shame rather than blame. It was time to draw a line under that period of German history and look forward. Schröder championed the admission of former communist countries into the European Union in order to end the division of Europe caused by the War; he declared the compensation of the Nazis' forced labourers to be a priority; and he was willing to commit German troops to combat operations abroad — in the Balkans and Afghanistan — something unthinkable under the previous guilt-ridden generation. Previous Chancellors had been more preoccupied with atonement: we saw Konrad Adenauer embrace Israel's founder, Ben-Gurion in 1966, Willy Brandt on his knees at a war memorial in Warsaw in

1970, and Helmut Kohl poignantly standing hand in hand with the French President François Mitterrand at the war cemetery at Verdun in 1984.

Atonement was very much a *West* German thing, however. In the communist east, from 1945 to 1989, there was a more simplistic — and less effective — way of dealing with the past. 'Anti-fascism' was the state policy of the German Democratic Republic (GDR), and like most communist state policies contained more wishful thinking than reality. East Germans were taught they had no need to feel blame for the past because *their government* had already taken care of all that: it had driven ex-Nazis out of the system (most of them were in any case living and thriving in the capitalist West), and the advance of socialism guaranteed they would not be revived. National socialism, so the doctrine went, had grown out of capitalism and could not, therefore, take root in the socialist East. Where *Wessis* were urged to 'overcome' the past, *Ossis* were not encouraged to face up to any individual responsibility for it. This led to a certain complacency in the East, and a failure to get to grips with the Nazi past in terms of national psychology.

This may be one reason why the revival of neo-Nazi and extreme-right groups in the nineties took place principally in the 'new *Länder*' — the eastern regions incorporated into the Federal Republic after the fall of the Berlin Wall. Few lessons from Germany's Nazi past had been drawn.

(In this sense, it was akin to Austria.) But there were other reasons too. East Germans had had far less contact with foreigners of any description throughout the forty years of communism. Few of them travelled abroad, and few foreign workers came to the East — unlike West Germany, where millions of mainly Turkish and Yugoslav *Gastarbeiter* had settled. Foreigners comprised only about 1 per cent of the GDR's population, and were not allowed to mix freely with local people. So on the one hand, the communist state had avoided the sporadic racial disturbances that West Germany experienced, but at the same time there was no need for East Germans to be schooled in the notion of 'respect for foreigners'. Whereas it was 'cool' for young Germans to live in Turkish quarters of West German cities, *Ossis* scarcely knew what a Doner kebab looked like.

Until, that is, the Wall came down, and they felt themselves competing with *Gastarbeiter* for scarce jobs. To complicate matters, within a year or so, the war in the former Yugoslavia caused the first major influx of refugees into Germany — and the eastern *Länder* were obliged to take in 20 per cent of them. A nation cocooned from the outside world suddenly found itself exposed to it — and discovered it was not a level playing field. Not only were there a lot of 'non-Germans' in the labour market, but East Germans themselves saw their economy slump into recession and unemployment. Jobless figures in the East quickly became twice as high as in the West, as inefficient state-run industries collapsed. The promise of prosperity dangled in front of them by West German politicians when the country was reunified in 1990 proved to be a mirage. Instead, for millions in the East, the future looked hopeless. Many people felt they had been rashly 'colonised' by the West: that feeling was reinforced, for example, during the East's first free elections, in the spring of 1990, which were dominated by high-publicity campaign trips carried out by *West* German politicians, above all Chancellor Helmut Kohl — the leader of a (still) foreign country campaigning in the East's elections *before reunification had even been decided upon*. Despite the efforts of many to promote a separate East German state, it was quickly gobbled up by the West, and all its traditions and values were unceremoniously trashed. Small wonder that populists and neo-Nazis found a welcome here.

Moreover, they were able to tap into a rebellious sub-culture which had existed even under — and probably because of — the restrictive conditions of the one-party communist state. The ban in the GDR on Nazi-style parties did not prevent small numbers of disaffected young people from adopting extreme right positions. From the early eighties disillusion with the rigid communist system, with its 'official' youth culture, began to find an outlet in various anti-Establishment forms, including skinhead and punk fashions and heavy metal music. Within a few years skinhead gangs and neo-Nazi groups known as *Faschos* began to proliferate, forming 'a distinct youth culture ... which adopted the Nazi convictions of German and Aryan superiority.'[3] Studies showed this first wave of extremists in the GDR to be mainly working-class, school-leavers or apprentices, with a low level of education. The fact that they could operate, semi-openly, in a police state like East Germany was perhaps surprising, but the fact that they developed at all should not have been. The GDR regime itself was authoritarian and anti-democratic, with an emphasis on state control and conformity, so it was an easy step for youngsters to shift their allegiances from a bankrupt 'left-wing' authoritarianism to an extreme right version — the more so since, contrary to the claims of the communist regime, the country had in any case not been truly purged of Nazism, and there had been no consistent attempt to understand the mistakes of the past. By 1988, 10-15 per cent of youth in the GDR apparently sympathised with Nazi ideology, while a survey at the time of reunification discovered 6 per cent in the East had very strongly anti-Semitic attitudes.[4]

Half-buried in GDR society, right-wing extremism suddenly broke into the open after the collapse of the communist system and the reunification of Germany. Perhaps this was part and parcel of the general release of pent-up potential, as people in the 'new *Länder*' found themselves free to explore avenues in politics, the economy and society that had been closed to them for forty years. Perhaps it was due to the specific insecurities faced by vulnerable sections of society in the suddenly imposed free-market conditions, or simply to the shock of the momentous transformation from a rigid, predictable system to a free-wheeling, unpredictable one. Whatever the reasons, the extreme right quickly became a more potent force in the East than in the West. The Federal Office for the Protection of the Constitution noted in a report: 'The peculiar historical and social situation in the New States gives rise to specific trends in right-wing extremism: a weakly developed party political presence is confronted with a disproportionately high readiness to use violence, when compared to the Old States. Although the population in the New States represents only 17 per cent of Germany's total population, some 45 percent of right-wing extremist motivated acts of violence are committed there.'[5]

∗

Alberto Adriano was a Mozambican who had lived in Dessau, a town of less than 100,000 people in eastern Germany, since arriving there as a 19-year-old student twenty years earlier. Now he worked in an abattoir. He and his German wife, Angelika, had three children:

Balarmino, 8, Manuel, 3, and a 5-month-old baby, Gabriel. On 11 June 2000, Whit Sunday, Adriano spent an evening at a friend's flat, watching football on television and discussing his forthcoming trip home to Mozambique, his first in five years, to see his parents and family. His flight was booked, and presents bought. He fell asleep in front of the television, and his friend covered him with a blanket. But when he woke up, at a quarter to two in the morning, Adriano took the fateful decision to go home — it was only a 400-metre walk across the park to his apartment block.

Even during the day the park is an unpleasant place. Surrounded by faceless Soviet-style housing blocks, it has a threatening air. Drunks and junkies lounge on benches, shady characters huddle in groups. On this warm summer night, as Adriano crossed the grass, three young men, skinheads, emerged from the shadows cast by the sodium streetlights. They had missed their trains home after a night of heavy drinking in Dessau, and were out looking for trouble, swaggering through the streets shouting fascist slogans. They were neo-Nazis, with previous convictions for wearing SS symbols in their haircuts and shouting 'Heil, Hitler!' from a balcony. Enrico Hilprecht, 25, and his two teenaged friends, Christian Richter and Frank Mietbauer, suddenly saw a chance to be of service to the Fatherland. They accosted Adriano with the words: 'What are you doing here in Germany?' Then they beat him to the ground, kicked him in the stomach, the head and the face, and stamped on him with their army-style boots, so hard and for so long that one of his eyes came out and he was left unconscious. A passer-by heard them laughing at their accomplishment. They later admitted to police that they had done it because they hated foreigners.

Adriano died in hospital three days later. A pink sandstone memorial now marks the spot where he was killed — the third that year alone to die in an extreme-right attack in Germany. I was in court to see the three killers sentenced. The younger ones smirked slightly as they were given juvenile terms of nine years in prison; they had the look of mindless youths who had never thought deeply about their beliefs — for whom, indeed, beliefs of any kind meant nothing. Hilprecht got life, and he looked as if he knew exactly what he believed in: a Germany free of foreigners, of blacks, of aliens, a Germany for Germans.

Foreigners like Adriano make up less than 2 per cent of Dessau's population, though the proportion could increase, as native Germans desert it in their tens of thousands. The town figures in European Union statistics as one of the poorest places in the whole of Europe: people here are five times worse off than their fellow citizens in Hamburg. The town is a collage of urban decay, a Lowry landscape with the smokestacks turned off. When I visited it a few years before Adriano's murder, I drove down rutted streets from one abandoned factory to another. On one street corner a local man pointed out to me a huge brewery — in Germany of all places — lying empty (taken over and then closed down, he said, by a huge West German concern). Across the road stood a deserted cement factory, and a paper works. 'It was the only factory in the GDR that made toilet paper,' the man told me ruefully, 'and they sold it off after reunification, and shipped the machines off the Africa.' For him, it was the ultimate insult: his former country now had to import bog paper — while Africans got the benefit of good German machinery.

The neighbouring city of Halle, birthplace of the composer Handel, boasts the highest unemployment in Germany — and the highest support for extreme right-wing parties. (The far-right *Deutschevolkunion* — the DVU — won 12.9 per cent of the vote in the state of Saxony-Anhalt, where both Dessau and Halle are situated, in elections to the state parliament in April 1998.) The vast housing estate known as Halle Neustadt illustrates how the GDR central planners' fetish for social engineering created a hothouse for extremism. More than 100,000 people were moved here to live in enormous chicken-coops erected in the sixties and seventies, with few amenities, to service chemical and other industries in the surrounding districts. Most of those industries collapsed after reunification, leaving tens of thousands of unemployed people, abandoned to idleness and drink. The only blessing is that

Crimes with Extreme Right Motivation

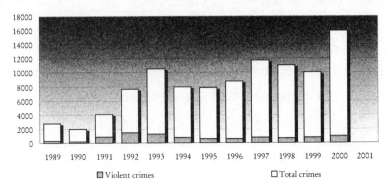

☐ Violent crimes   ☐ Total crimes

Membership of Extreme Right-Wing Groups

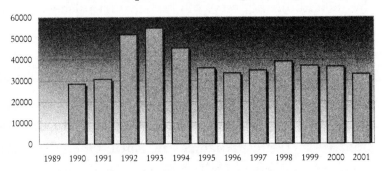

Asylum-seekers in Germany

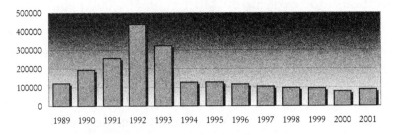

Sources: Bundesamt für Verfassungsschutz; UNHCR.

the closure of the chemical factories has ended some of Europe's worst pollution. The people of Saxony-Anhalt have clean air and rivers now, but no hope of much else.

A local radio journalist showed me round the desolate canyons of Halle Neustadt — 20-storey blocks with porthole windows, broken glass and urine in every doorway, small boys smoking, men scarcely capable of standing but gripping their beer bottles tight, all vowing to vote for the far right or — joke — the German Beer Drinkers' Party.

In another dismal town, Wolfen-Nord, where two of Alberto Adriano's killers came from, there is a youth club, which you approach through an empty car park choked with weeds breaking through the tarmac. On its roof stands a worthless Trabant car — the 'Trabi', the fibre-glass jalopy that was the ubiquitous means of transport in 1989-90, when thousands of East Germans made their first excited trips to the West, now stuck on top of a youth club in the middle of a post-industrial wasteland, a symbol of hopelessness and disorientation.

Adriano's murder caused a wave of revulsion throughout Germany because of its particular brutality. But it was not new. As the tables show, violent crimes attributed by the German police to right-wing extremism picked up from about 1991 — a year after reunification. There would appear to be a correlation too between the numbers of asylum seekers coming to Germany and both the incidence of far-right crime (including the spreading of neo-Nazi propaganda and racist literature) and the membership of far-right parties. Immigration reached a peak in 1992, and both extremist crimes and party membership rose dramatically in 1992-93. There was a second rise in both phenomena in the late eighties, when the Kosovo crisis brought fears of further immigration and a *real* increase (not reflected in the official asylum seeker figures) of illegal immigration.

As noted earlier, most of these acts of racial violence occurred in the new eastern states, despite their smaller population. They began with a spate of attacks against hostels for asylum seekers at the beginning of the decade, in such places as Rostock and Hoyerswerda. Leipzig, where huge peaceful demonstrations in 1989 helped to bring down the communist regime, later became a hotbed of racism. Dr Atiqur Rahman, an Indian scientist, had only been in the city a few hours when skinheads dragged him from a telephone kiosk as he attempted to call home. They smashed his spectacles, kicked him to the ground and set a dog on him. They left him bleeding from an inch-deep bite in his arm. Rahman had come to Leipzig on an academic exchange programme to work with German colleagues on an environmental project.

In Weimar, cradle of German culture, I met skinheads who spoke about their ambition to create a Greater Germany and 'correct the wrongs' committed against their

Fatherland. They wanted things that no political party was even offering — the return of Germans expelled after the War from the Sudetenland and Silesia, the reincorporation into Germany of land ceded to Poland, the return of 'Danzig' (Gdansk). Some even wanted Ukraine and Russia 'back'. These were bored young men (and girls), unemployed, and with — I sensed — not much more knowledge of Hitler than of Goethe and Schiller, near whose monument we were standing. They said they supported the far-right DVU, but their politics appeared to be drawn less from any real understanding of German history than from the lyrics of the songs they heard at neo-Nazi concerts.

The German police have identified skinhead music and the Internet as primary means of 'agitation' used by the extreme right. A conference organised by the Federal Criminal Office in June 2002 heard how 'hatred is engendered through the medium of music with racist, anti-Semitic and often violence-glorifying words. A sense of community and strength is encouraged by attending skinhead concerts.'[6] A publication of the Federal Office for the Protection of the Constitution included the following sample of skinhead lyrics:

> *Ich mag Adolf und sein Reich,*
> *Alle Juden sind mir gleich.*
> *Ich mag Skinheads und SA,*

Türken klatschen, ist doch klar.
Ich mag Fußball auf dem Rasen,
Die SS, wenn sie gasen.
All das mag ich, und ganz doll NSDAP.

I like Adolf and his Reich, don't give a
    damn about Jews.
I like skinheads and the SA
    (Stormtroopers), and beating up
    Turks of course.
I like football on the grass, and the SS
    when they're using gas.
I like all that, and first of all the
    NSDAP (Nazi Party)

Police action in the early nineties kept skinhead bands and concerts to a minimum, but since the beginning of 1997 they have been proliferating, many of them attracting a thousand or more participants. Audiences demand the performance of xenophobic songs with titles such as 'The Africa Song', 'Ali the Turk' and 'Dreck muß weg (Filth must be swept out)'. An anti-Semitic song from the twenties, entitled 'Blood must flow', has been revived and is performed by many skinhead bands. It includes the following verse:

Wetzt die langen Messer auf dem Bürgersteig;

Laßt die Messer flutschen in den Judenleib.
Blut muß fließen knüppelhageldick,
Und wir scheißen auf die Freiheit dieser
 Judenrepublik.

Sharpen the long knives on the pavement;
Stick them in a Jewish body.
Blood must flow, thick and deep,
And we shit on the freedom of this Jewish
 republic.

The concerts are organised by neo-Nazi groups such as Blood & Honour and Hammerskins (which originated in Britain and America) and also by the National Democratic Party (NPD) which has found them a useful way of attracting young people to its ranks. The Internet has become the most common means both of advertising concerts and of spreading fascist propaganda whose open publication would be prohibited.

٭

Besides the NPD, two other far-right political parties are active in Germany today — the Republikaner (REP) and the German People's Union (DVU). Formed in 1964, the NPD is the oldest and most extreme of them — though not its most influential. It claims to adhere to the democratic principle that political power must be won only through parliamentary work, but at the same time it actively recruits neo-Nazis and skinheads, who give its rallies and demonstrations a menacing, militant air. Its membership had dropped to a low of 3,500 in 1996, but since the election that year of Udo Voigt as its leader, membership has almost doubled. The party's ideology is racist and xenophobic, claiming the existence of a 'national community' based on 'common biological features'. It refuses to accept a 'multicultural society' which it says is synonymous with a 'multicriminal' society. It advocates that foreigners be repatriated rather than integrated, and excluded from Germany's social welfare system. The party programme demands a 'fundamental political change [which] must end the misanthropic policy of integration and maintain the substance of the German people [*Volkssubstanz*].' It also states that 'Germany is bigger than the Federal Republic' and demands the revision of the country's borders which were agreed after the War.[7]

In the summer of 2000, when public opinion was incensed by the murder of Alberto Adriano and a bomb explosion in Dusseldorf which injured ten immigrants, the social-democratic government of Chancellor Schröder decided to push for a ban on the NPD because of its association with far-right violence — subject to consideration by the Constitutional Court of the legality of such a move, and despite fears that it could be driven underground or even gain in popularity. Asked whether this was not taking a sledgehammer to a crack a nut, interior minister Otto Schily said: 'Hitler and his associates were once just a tiny group and one could have said it would have been disproportionate to ban the Nazi party back then.'[8]

Pressure to impose the ban increased after the terrorist attacks of September 11th, when the NPD issued an inflammatory television advertisement (which no station screened) predicting a future of discord and violence in Germany if it supported America, and staged its first protest march through West Berlin. The party's lawyer, Horst Mahler, condoned the attacks on the World Trade Centre and the Pentagon: 'I would say it was a military operation of the oppressed people in the Arab world, and it is justified warfare against these global structures centred in Washington and New York. This is a goal for all people in the world, and therefore they have my sympathy — even though it is true that the death of thousands of people is a cruel act. But it is a war and war is always cruel.'[9]

The government's campaign ended in disarray, however, when it emerged in 2002 that nine senior NPD members whose racist statements were a key part of the case against it had been paid government informants, working for the Office for the Protection of the Constitution. The government was made to look, in the words of the *Frankfurter Allgemeine Zeitung*, 'idiotic'. Wolfgang Frenz, a co-founder of the NPD, and Udo

Holtmann, publisher of the party's newspaper, had received government money for their intelligence work for decades, and donated much of it to the party — meaning the Office for the Protection of the Constitution had been subsidising one of its principal enemies. In May the Constitutional Court postponed its hearing until October — making it possible for the NPD to field candidates in the general election in September.

The NPD's impact on elections so far has been negligible, while the Republikaner and the DVU have occasionally scored alarmingly high results. In 1989 the Republikaner scored 7.1 per cent in elections to the European Parliament, and in 1992 gained seats in a regional parliament for the first time, winning 10.9 per cent of the vote in the West German state of Baden-Württemberg. That was their high-point and the success has not been repeated. The DVU did better in the new *Länder*. In April 1998 it won an astonishing 12.9 per cent in Saxony-Anhalt. But none of the parties were strong enough to make headway in the federal elections later that year: the Republikaner won 1.8 per cent, the DVU 1.2 per cent, and the NPD just 0.3 per cent.

The Republikaner was formed in 1983 by three former members of the mainstream conservative CSU (Christian Social Union — the Bavarian version of the CDU). Two of them, Franz Handlos and Ekkehard Voigt, had been members of the Bundestag, while the third, Franz

Schönhuber, was a former member of the Nazi party and Waffen-SS. The party grew to around 14,000 members. It is regarded as the most 'moderate' of the three far-right parties — akin to the National Front in France or the Freedom Party in Austria — and its federal chairman, a lawyer, Rolf Schlierer, is keen to present it as a respectable conservative right-wing movement. It is xenophobic and anti-Semitic, however, and plays down the crimes of the Nazis. It demands an end to immigration to 'stop Germans becoming foreigners in their own land'.

The DVU came into being in Munich in 1971 and is now the largest far-right party in Germany with a (declining) membership of around 17,000. It is dominated by its founder and chairman, the publisher Gerhard Frey, thanks to his financial strength and authoritarian regime. The Federal Office for the Protection of the Constitution describes the DVU's central ideology as 'extreme and chauvinistic nationalism'.[10] The party identifies itself first and foremost with Germany and the German nation, and its policies focus on the protection of German society from 'anti-German' forces. Frey's publishing house and newspaper (the *National-Zeitung — Deutsche Wochenzeitung*) are used to propagate his views, which the authorities regard as being directed 'against the free democratic basic order', while conceding that 'it will be extremely difficult to prove that the party's profile is characterised by aggressiveness and militancy.'

Studies of the DVU's remarkable success in 1998, when it won 16 seats in the regional parliament of Saxony-Anhalt, suggest it attracted many protest voters, dissatisfied with growing unemployment (which reached 25 per cent in the region that year) and disillusioned by the failure of mainstream parties to make it prosper in unified Germany. The majority of those who voted for the DVU were not themselves right-wing extremists: they included neo-Nazis but also people who were in search of new political directions. The party does not have a large or stable extreme-right core to draw on, making it vulnerable to the ups and downs of the economic and political climate.[11] Its future success could thus depend to a large extent on how the mainstream parties appear to be dealing with social and economic problems. Only six months after its success at regional level, the federal elections of October 1998 saw the DVU's vote in Saxony-Anhalt drop to just 3.2 per cent.

Together, the NPD, Republikaner and DVU gained 4.6 per cent of the vote in the 1998 Bundestag election, but so long as they remain disunited none of them looks at all likely to cross the 5 per cent threshold to enter the Bundestag. So far the leaders of the three parties have rejected suggestions of electoral pacts or other forms of co-operation, so they cannot be seen as a real threat at national level.

In 2001 attention focused on a new populist, anti-immigration party which emerged in the city-state of

Hamburg in the wake of the September 11th terrorist attacks on New York and Washington and swept up about 20 per cent of the vote in elections to the city government. Hamburg has a large number of immigrants — in the early nineties it took in as many as the total number accepted by the United Kingdom — and the new party benefited from a wave of fear following the discovery that some of the suicide hijackers had lived in the city. The so-called *Partei Rechtstaatlicher Offensive* (Law and Order Party) was led by a 43-year-old former judge, Ronald Schill, dubbed 'Judge Merciless' because of the severe sentences he used to hand down. His party joined a centre-right coalition in the city administration, with Schill himself becoming 'Innensenator' (interior minister) with responsibility for justice and the police. He is an intensely controversial figure. One of his early proposals was to offer African countries up to €8,300 (£5,200) a head to accept rejected asylum seekers — regardless of their nationality. This represented the annual cost, he claimed, of keeping illegal immigrants in the city. He also launched a crack-down on drug-abuse, in a city with more than two thousand dealers and a soaring crime rate. One initiative was to administer forced emetics to suspected drugs-traffickers — to discover whether they might have swallowed their goods fearing arrest. One suspect died from the procedure.

Schill himself was not at first inclined to contest the federal elections in 2002, but his party persuaded him to do so. His campaign was badly damaged, however, by a scandalous scene in the Bundestag just weeks before polling day. Schill used his right as a Hamburg city senator to address a debate on the summer's severe flooding in Germany. The debate was intended to demonstrate cross-party unity on restoring the damaged regions, but Schill launched a crude attack on the government's policies on taxation and immigration. He overran his allotted time, had his microphone cut by the Speaker, and then threatened to complain to the Federal Constitutional Court. It was a ruinous miscalculation. His xenophobic remarks caused an uproar. Chancellor Schröder warned of the growing threat of right-wing populism. 'The Schills,' he said, 'are not confined to Hamburg.' Members of Schill's own party disowned him, and his popularity slumped even in his Hamburg stronghold. In the election in September, his party polled less than one per cent. Once again, Germany's far right had proved inept in the art of politics.

*

German governments have taken various steps over the past decade or so to deal both directly with extremist organisations and with the factors believed to lie behind them. Intense surveillance of neo-Nazi groups, including their websites and concerts, has been backed up with outright bans on several organisations: between 1992 and 2000 eighteen groups were outlawed. There have also been moves to restrict the influx of asylum seekers by limiting their right of appeal and making their expulsion or repatriation easier. Joint European Union action to curb illegal immigration is strongly supported by Germany, which has received far more incomers than any other EU country.

At the same time, however, Germany became the first European country to introduce a 'green card' scheme to attract skilled workers, particularly in the field of information technology, from India and other developing countries. The measure, brought in by Chancellor Schröder's government in 2000, was seen as essential to fill a growing skills gap and also to create a larger workforce paying into state pension schemes for the benefit of a growing, ageing population. It was not a great success, however, and a new immigration law, passed in March 2002, went further. Abandoning the principle of accepting as permanent immigrants only people with strong blood ties, the law granted highly-qualified foreigners immediate entry, for an indefinite period. Others would be admitted according to a system of points, awarded according to criteria such as age, qualifications and knowledge of German. All new residents were required to follow an 'integration course', including German language and history. The interior minister, Otto Schily, described it as 'the most modern immigration legislation in Europe: with this law, Germany shows itself to be an open country.' Not everyone was convinced. The Nobel Prize-winning writer Günther Grass condemned the government for distinguishing between 'useful' asylum seekers and those who would be a burden on the taxpayer: 'This system of selection is called "Selektieren", a word which harks back to a criminal national past,' he said, referring to Nazi racial policies. Grass said thousands of asylum seekers were held in detention in Germany pending deportation, 'as though they were criminals'.[12]

Immigration inevitably became a major issue in the 2002 Bundestag election campaign, with the conservative opposition candidate for Chancellor, Bavarian premier Edmund Stoiber, promising to reverse the new law and take even tougher action against bogus asylum-seekers. He insisted the mainstream parties had to address the issue to prevent the far right from scoring political points, but his own language echoed the far right's, suggesting that allowing immigration was not compatible with fighting unemployment. He said schools and ordinary citizens were already struggling with the 'heavy additional burden' of integrating foreigners into society. 'And the government plans to allow more immigration. Our society can't cope with this. Germany needs to limit and regulate immigration.' Some years earlier, Stoiber (who had encouraged the Austrian conservative leader, Wolfgang Schüssel, to go into coalition with Jörg Haider) warned against the 'tainting of the German race' by immigrants. Just days before the election he went even further, pledging to expel 4,000 Islamic militants, who, he said, 'are known by name to the police as being disposed to violence and are suspected of belonging to foreign terrorist organisations.'

It remains to be seen whether the adoption of stricter immigration policies and the improvement of the economy, especially in the new *Länder*, will diminish the hard right's influence. The existence of skinhead violence, as a fringe phenomenon, seems likely to continue, however, and there is little the authorities can do to prevent the far right from regrouping. It emerged in May 2002 that a leading neo-Nazi, Steffen Hupka, was setting up a training school in the grounds of a castle near the city of Halle. *Stern* magazine reported that large seminar rooms, a beer garden and flats for far-right holidaymakers were being planned.

Germans, meanwhile, remain deeply scarred by the Nazi past, even though almost six decades have passed since the War. No other nation is so sensitive to accusations of anti-Semitism. Indeed, it is almost impossible to have a neutral discussion of Middle East politics in Germany: can a German criticise Israel without being labelled an anti-Semite? Several incidents in 2002 demonstrated the extent to which a generation of Germans which had nothing whatsoever to do with Nazism remains saddled with its legacy.

The deputy leader of the mainstream Liberal party (FDP), Jürgen Möllemann, was forced to apologise after a row over the right to criticise Israel descended into abusive exchanges between Möllemann and a senior German Jewish leader. Referring to Palestinian suicide bombers in Israel, Möllemann said: 'I too would resist, indeed violently.' He also supported an application to join the party by a Syrian-born German politician named Jamal Karsli, who had accused the Israeli army of 'Nazi methods' and complained of the influence of the Zionist lobby in the media. This prompted fierce criticism from Michel Friedman, a somewhat abrasive television talk show host who happens to be deputy head of Germany's Central Council of Jews. Instead of backing down, Möllemann retorted that it was precisely people like Friedman 'with his intolerant and spiteful manner' and the Israeli prime minister, Ariel Sharon, who were causing the rise of anti-Semitism in Germany. Friedman's boss, the head of the Central Council of Jews, Paul Spiegel, said that was 'the worst insult delivered to Jews in the name of a political party since the Holocaust', while the *Washington Post* was incensed by what it called 'these vile but carefully crafted appeals', which it took as proof of 'the sad reality that anti-Semitism has no more died away in Europe than racism has in the United States, and though no serious European politicians now accept the discriminatory agendas of the past, much less the genocide of the Nazis, the ancient prejudice nevertheless is alive in electoral politics and may twist some of the debate about the Middle East.'[13] Möllemann won praise — doubtless to his dismay — from Jörg Haider.

At around the same time a distinguished German author, Martin Walser, found himself at the centre of a row over allegations of anti-Semitism after the *Frankfurter Allgemeine Zeitung* refused to serialise his latest book. The author had earlier provoked controversy by saying the Holocaust was being exploited and that Auschwitz must not be used as a 'tool of intimidation, a moral cudgel'. His new book, *Death of a Critic*, which deals with the suspected murder of a Jewish literary critic, was condemned as being full of anti-Semitic clichés.

The Möllemann affair and the Walser book controversy are much more than dinner-table talk among the chattering classes. They are symptoms of a German malaise, an inability, after all these years, to shed the burden of history. A younger generation of Germans would love to be 'normal' — to have no hang-ups about an increasingly distant past, and to have the right, for example, to discuss Israeli politics as people in other European countries do, without risking accusations of anti-Semitism. But political correctness is even more restrictive in Germany than elsewhere in Europe. No other nation is so called upon to exhibit moral rectitude. It is an unwelcome fetter on those who feel unfairly tainted by association with their grandfathers — but it may also ensure that German governments continue to clamp down successfully on far-right extremism, lest anyone suspect the old genie is about to re-emerge from the bottle.

Notes

1   *Verfassungsschutzbericht 2001.*

2   *Tagesspiegel Online*, 14 September 2000.

3   Susann Backer, 'Right-Wing Extremism in Unified Germany', in *The Politics of the Extreme Right* (ed. Paul Hainsworth), London: Pinter, 2000, p. 103.

4   *Ibid.*, p. 104.

5   Bundesamt für Verfassungsschutz, 'Trends in Right-Wing Extremism in the New Federal States', January 1999.

6   Press release of the *Bundeskriminalamt*, 20 June 2002.

7   NPD Party Programme

8   BBC News, 8 November 2000.

9   BBC News, 3 October 2001.

[10] Bundesamt für Verfassungsschutz, 'Right-wing Extremism in Germany', September 2000.

[11] Susann Backer, *op. cit.*, p. 107.

[12] Günter Grass, 'No Voice,' speech to the European Conference against Racism 'All different, All Equal' Strasbourg 10/2000.

[13] *Washington Post*, 17 June 2002.

4.

The Browning of France

If Jean-Marie Le Pen is the brash public face of the French hard right, Maxime Brunerie is the quiet, hidden, terrifying cancer at its heart. Born in 1977, five years after Le Pen founded the *Front national*, Brunerie grew up in the southern Paris suburb of Courcouronnes, a supporter of the Paris Saint-Germain football club and later an accountancy student. There was nothing about his behaviour to alert neighbours to his extremist views — but he kept neo-Nazi literature, including a copy of *Mein Kampf*, in his bedroom, and the police had kept a file on him since the age of 18 because of his association with extreme right groups, including PSG's Kop de Boulogne supporters group — an alliance of skinheads and far-right hooligans who regularly caused trouble at matches.

Brunerie himself did not have a police record, but he was active in several extremist associations. He joined the *Mouvement national républicain* (MNR), the far-right party formed by Bruno Mégret when he broke away from Le Pen's National Front in 1999, and became a candidate for it in local elections in March 2001 — number seven on its list for the 18th arrondissement of Paris. He was also a member of the neo-Nazi *Unité radicale*, and edited a skinhead fanzine, *Rebelle blanc*. He had links with the *Parti nationaliste français européen* (PNFE), a neo-fascist organisation which holds annual banquets to celebrate Adolf Hitler's birthday, and with the *Groupement union défense* (GUD), an ultra-right student group whose members like to demonstrate by the statue of Joan of Arc in Paris wearing face-masks and black leather jackets and gloves. PNFE sympathisers are suspected of fire-bombing immigrant hostels in the south of France and of desecrating a Jewish cemetery. Two of its members have been convicted. One of its pamphlets claims, 'at Treblinka, only lice were gassed', and its website sells stickers with the slogans 'Tolerate immigrants? Never!' and 'We no longer feel at home in our homeland.' In the GUD, Brunerie was said to have been responsible for maintaining contacts with far-right rock bands — a relatively benign occupation in a group that is violently anti-Semitic: its members fired tear-gas in a Paris cinema showing *Shoah*, a documentary about the Holocaust, and set fire to the offices of left-wing and pro-Palestinian groups.

Brunerie attended a reception held by Mégret's MNR after the first round of the 2002 presidential election, in which the far right had scored its best ever success. He attracted the attention of a reporter from *Le Monde*, who quoted him as saying he would vote for Le Pen in the second round, though he complained the National Front was 'adrift', that is, not extreme enough for his liking.[1] Le Pen was trounced by President Jacques Chirac in the second round, and — whether there was a causal link or not remains unclear — Brunerie decided to take things into his own hands. On 6 July he bought a .22 rifle — the first firearm he had ever owned — and drew up careful plans. He posted a message on the English-language website of the Combat 18 movement, suggesting far-right colleagues should 'watch the television this Sunday. I will be the star.' The '18' in the movement's name refers to the first and eighth letters of the alphabet, AH — Adolf Hitler. Brunerie ended his message: 'Death to zog, 88!' which in neo-Nazi parlance means 'Death to the Zionist occupation government, Heil Hitler!' On Bastille Day, the 14th, he packed his new gun into a guitar case, drove a hired car into Paris, and took up a position in the crowd lining the pavements near the Champs Elysées, where Chirac was due to pass in an open-top jeep. As the president neared,

Brunerie took out his gun and fired. Chirac was saved only by the would-be assassin's cackhandedness and the courage of bystanders who wrestled him to the ground and grabbed the gun. In police custody later, Brunerie told psychiatrists he had 'a profound hatred of Jacques Chirac and of democracy' and that he had intended to kill the president.

Brunerie's attempted assassination may well have been due more to mental instability than to his political views, and there was no indication that he was acting at the behest of any of the extremist groups with which he had links — any more than the animal-rights activist who killed Pim Fortuyn in Holland two months earlier was acting on behalf of any organisation — but the two incidents brought the spectre of political murder to the very forefront of European politics. From now on the Establishment would have to think not just about tighter security for its leading politicians, but about the emergence of a new factor in far-right politics — the incubation of a crazed, murderous virus in the hothouse of hate.

And after all, violence is never far beneath the surface on the extreme right, including the *Front national*, despite Le Pen's desire to make it respectable. Its leader has always exuded an air of menace: he lost an eye in a street brawl during the parliamentary election of 1950, and hit a female candidate in 1997; Front supporters shot an immigrant dead in 1995, three were jailed for murdering a Muslim teenager in Marseille in 1998, while others threw a North

African to his death from a Paris bridge during a party rally. And this is the party which was too soft for Maxime Brunerie.

*

There were two ways to look at the spectacular success of Jean-Marie Le Pen in the first round of the 2002 presidential election. On the one hand, his 16.86 per cent of the vote — knocking out the socialist prime minister Lionel Jospin, and proceeding to a second-round run-off against President Jacques Chirac — was an aberration: his share of the vote was up by less than 2 per cent on the previous election seven years earlier (and by only 134,000 actual votes), and he would not have come second if the left had not been split among several candidates. When it came to the next round a massive 82 per cent of French voters demonstrated they had no time for his brand of extreme-right, xenophobic populism. Le Pen will be 78 by the time of the next election and is thus unlikely to repeat even that qualified success.

On the other hand, five million French men and women did vote for some of the most illiberal, racist, anti-European, nationalistic and mean-minded policies on offer in Europe today. Surveys suggest an even greater number of French people actually share many of Le Pen's views, but either could not bring themselves to vote for him, or felt that President Jacques Chirac, if re-elected, would do the job anyway. In certain regions and cities support for Le Pen and his National Front party is prodigious. And even if Le Pen himself goes into decline, his ideas have been around, gathering momentum and bitterness, for many years and are unlikely to recede.

He portrays himself, like all populist leaders, as a man of the people — their defence against a corrupt, mainstream establishment that is watering down the essence of France, selling it off to the multinationals and Brussels, their defence against foreigners, and against the crime and unemployment they allegedly cause in France. The National Front website is full of pictures of Jean-Marie: always smiling, crinkly-eyed, casually dressed in open-necked shirts and stylish pullovers, sometimes with his young wife (his new one, Jany, not the previous one who took her clothes off for *Playboy* to embarrass him) leaning on his shoulder as he stands at the helm of their yacht, or cuddling their pet dog. There is Le Pen the fisherman's son, the miner, the 'man of action' in charge of a student brigade to help Dutch flood victims in 1953, the paratrooper in Indochina, the youngest MP in the National Assembly, the volunteer fighting 'for the defence of French Algeria', Le Pen with the Pope, with Reagan, with black African presidents. He is the family man, the grandfather, the man who will save France from 'immigration, unemployment, AIDS and the decrease of the birth rate [which] pose a real threat to the liberty and security of the French people and to the very survival of France.' The website continues: 'The *Front national*, an assembly of patriotic, lucid and courageous men and women, embodies the fight against decadence. Today, it is the only hope for the French people.' No doubts about that, then: it is the survival of the French nation that is at stake, and the avuncular M. Le Pen is the man to ensure it. Yet for such a French Frenchman, his brand of politics is not about those ancient virtues of *liberté, égalité, fraternité*. If anything, rather the opposite, on all three counts.

Le Pen's egregious statements about the Holocaust ('a detail of history') and race ('some races are more equal than others') are routinely cited by his opponents. Few can forget his physical assault on a woman candidate in 1997, for which he was banned from public office for a year. But it is Le Pen's rallies that give the best flavour of his demagogic style and behaviour. He likes to enter the stage to the sound of thunderous triumphal music and the cheering of thousands of fans, which he acknowledges with raised arms, like an Olympic champion. He can hold his audience for hours, pacing the stage, telling jokes, threading his way masterfully from one national prejudice to the next, tapping into his audience's insecurities, about crime, law and order, unemployment, whatever, responding to their laughter like a top-class stand-up comedian and to their anger like a priest — calming, comforting, reassuring. His political points are peppered with anecdotes — the immigrant family he just heard of, who're scrounging on welfare while their French neighbours live in poverty, the good French trader defeated by some absurd new Brussels law... And always that simple, insidious equation: three million unemployed equals three million immigrants. What could be easier: chuck 'em out and save France for the French. His audiences are rapt, rising to the swell of his patriotic fervour, cheering as he invokes France's beauty and greatness and exhorts them to 'defend her, rebuild her!'

Le Pen's policies are sublimely simplistic, with scarcely a thought, it seems, to their practicality. He proposes, for example, four steps to 'reverse the tide of immigration'. One, establish the 'national and European preference' in all areas — accommodation, employment, social welfare. In other words, houses, jobs and benefits should go to French people and (white) Europeans first. Two, immediate expulsion of all immigrants in an 'irregular situation', that is of all incomers who are not yet legally registered. (In fact, he has often indicated a desire to deport all foreigners, illegal or not.) Three, end all family reunification — so even legal immigrants would no longer be able to bring in their spouses, children or parents. And four, abolish the automatic right to French nationality.

The European Union — into which France is meshed by thousands of treaty articles and laws, not to mention by trade and customs — can almost be wished away. Le Pen would 'annul the treaties of Maastricht, Schengen and Amsterdam', abrogate the constitutional amendment allowing foreigners to vote, and 'abolish the Brussels Commission' — just like that![2]

Other policies combine brutal discrimination with a kind of egalitarianism — for the French. On health, for instance, Le Pen says there should be separate funds for French people and foreigners, and that all French people should enjoy identical social protection. Income tax would be 'progressively abolished' — leaving VAT as the government's main source of revenue.

France under Le Pen would become inward looking and isolated. He proposes a 'new protectionism', with trade barriers 'to protect our jobs and our products'. There would be state aid to help firms 'reconquer' the internal market.

Immigration is clearly Le Pen's overriding preoccupation — but it is not a single issue, rather a prism through which all other problems are refracted, with the immigrant made a scapegoat for society's ills. Whether the problem is urban crime or high unemployment, the declining birthrate or France's cultural purity, AIDS, drugs or falling educational standards, it can generally be blamed on foreigners, particularly Muslims and particularly those from the Maghreb, north-west Africa. The European Union and globalisation cannot, of course, be blamed on immigrants, but they are blamed for having the same deleterious effect on France — reducing its sanctity as a nation state, diluting the Frenchness of France.

Joan of Arc is the Front's heroine and mascot — the fifteenth-century Maid of Orleans who led her followers in battle against the English, but was denounced as a heretic and burned at the stake, a martyr. Le Pen, too, likes to play the martyr. After his triumph in the first round of the 2002 presidential election he went to the European Parliament in Brussels, apparently to use it as a platform to air his anti-EU policies. He made a perfunctory speech on foreign policy in the chamber — exercising his rights as a member — but this was just a prelude to the planned main event, a news conference aimed at maximum publicity on the evening news at home and abroad. Hundreds of journalists and scores of cameramen packed the hall, plus a few members of parliament armed with posters saying 'Non!' which they intended to brandish during his appearance. We waited ... and waited. After an hour and a half Le Pen's representative appeared to explain to the furious, sweating press corps that the leader was cancelling his news conference 'because the hall is full of hostile MEPs who want to cause a disorder'. It was the lamest excuse one could have imagined. French journalists pointed out that it was probably the effect Le Pen wished to achieve: here he was, a member of the European Parliament, deprived by euro-stooges of his constitutional right to address the public — burned, as it were, at the Brussels stake.

✳

Born in 1928 in Brittany, Jean-Marie Le Pen began his political career in the fifties as president of a right-wing student group while studying law at Paris University. After an interlude fighting in Vietnam he returned to France and joined the far-right Poujadist Movement, which in 1956 won 52 seats in the National Assembly — including one in Rennes for Le Pen, who became parliament's youngest ever deputy. He interrupted his parliamentary career two years later to join the army again, this time as a parachutist in Algeria, fighting against the independence movement (and reportedly torturing prisoners). Back in France, he was arrested for political extremism in 1960, failed to win a parliamentary seat in 1962, and sank for some years into obscurity.

His ambitions never wavered, though, and in October 1972 he became head of the new National Front, created by activists in a revolutionary-nationalist group known as the *Ordre nouveau*. The new party brought together several strands of right-wing, nationalist politics. At this stage, immigration was not an issue: the party's programme called for the dismantling of the 'ubiquitous state', including the public sector, it defended the interests of small businessmen, supported the dictatorships in Spain, Greece and Portugal, and was generally pro-American and anti-communist. For more than a decade it had little impact.

During this period Le Pen worked as a printer, but in 1976 he was bequeathed a fortune — 20 million francs and a grand red-brick mansion in the Saint Cloud suburb of Paris — by an industrialist, Hubert Lambert, who changed his will in Le Pen's favour just nine months before he died of drink. The circumstances of this inheritance caused controversy, when an old ally of Le Pen's, Jean Demarquet, claimed that Le Pen had exerted undue influence over Lambert as he lay dying.[3] Whatever the truth, the cash gave Le Pen all the financial independence he could wish for to pursue his political ambitions. Within a few years it bore fruit.

In 1983 the Front's Jean-Pierre Stirbois scored a spectacular 16.7 per cent in the first round of local elections in the town of Dreux after a campaign that included the shocking populist line: 'Immigrants from beyond the Mediterranean — go back to your huts!' In response to Stirbois' success, the centre-right party in Dreux then merged with the Front for the second round, thereby conferring upon it the legitimacy it craved. Le Pen was quick to capitalise on this, and in the European elections the following year, the National Front at last burst out of obscurity to become a major and lasting force in French politics. It won 11 per cent of the vote and 10 seats in the Strasbourg parliament, after campaigning on a platform increasingly dominated by the question of immigration. In 1986 the Front's 9.7 per cent gave it 35 seats in the National Assembly — a freak result, never repeated, due to the fact that the socialist president François Mitterrand had introduced a proportional voting system: in later parliamentary elections Le Pen's party won more votes but never more than a single seat, as a two-round first-past-the-post system was reintroduced.

By now Le Pen had begun an intensive recruitment drive, attracting rising stars from the moderate and nationalist right, including Bruno Mégret from President Jacques Chirac's RPR party, who was to manage Le Pen's presidential campaign in 1988. The party's policies began to change subtly, to recognise the fact that many of the social policies pursued under Mitterrand — such as the 39-hour week and a fifth week of paid holidays — were popular with the workers, a constituency which Le Pen wanted to break into. He toned down his criticism of the welfare state and the public sector, and had supporters campaign at factory gates in an attempt to win the working-class vote. Mégret himself toured factories, stirring things up and systematically infiltrating trade unions or even setting up parallel unions — in, for example, the police and prisons service. It was a tactic adopted from the old Communist Party, from which the

Front gradually stole more and more supporters, becoming by the mid-nineties the foremost working-class party in France, with some 30 per cent of workers' votes and 25 per cent among the unemployed. The Front also began creating an 'extended family' of 'circles' and satellite organisations, ranging from its youth wing, the *Front national de la Jeunesse*, to the benign-sounding 'Hunting, Fishing and Nature Circle', the 'Front against Unemployment', the 'National Circle of Women of Europe' and 'SOS Children of Iraq'. There is even a 'National Circle of French Jews' and a 'National Circle of Taxis' — all run by the National Front. It also runs summer schools and magazines.

It was in a television interview in September 1987 that Le Pen first remarked that the Nazi gas chambers were a mere 'detail' of the history of the Second World War. It did him no harm. The following year 4.4 million voters cast their ballots for him in the presidential election (in which Mitterrand was re-elected). Le Pen's 14.4 per cent share of the vote was a triumph, and may have encouraged him to believe that outrageous racist or anti-Semitic comments could only help him. In 1988 he caused further offence with a punning reference to the gas chambers, when he referred to a Jewish minister in the socialist government, Michel Durafour (*four* means 'oven'), as 'Monsieur Durafour-crématoire'. Two leading members of his party resigned in protest, but Le Pen barged on regardless. In 1990 he was convicted of incitement to racial hatred after casting doubt on the Nazis' persecution of Jews and gypsies, and fined the equivalent of FF 1.2m ($233.000). (When he repeated the allegations in Munich in 1997 he ran foul of Germany's hate speech laws.)

The early nineties saw the Front making a systematic attempt to build up its support by codifying its hardline and xenophobic policies in easily digestible forms. Under the guidance of the party's main strategist, Bruno Mégret, it published a document entitled *Immigration: Fifty Concrete Measures* in 1991, and a new party programme, *300 Measures for the Renaissance of France*, in 1993. Central to both was the *préférence nationale* — the policy of giving priority to French people in every field of life. Le Pen proposed incorporating the principle into a new Constitution if he became president.

The strategy yielded startling results in a series of elections. In 1992 the Front won 13.9 per cent of the vote, and 239 seats, in regional elections. In 1993 it had its best ever showing in National Assembly elections — 12.7 per cent (though no seats, thanks to the electoral system). In 1994 eleven National Front deputies entered the European Parliament. And in 1995 Le Pen scored 15.5 per cent in the presidential elections (which were won by Jacques Chirac). That year also saw more than a thousand local councillors elected, and the Front took control of three southern towns — Toulon, Orange and Marignane (an industrial centre near Marseille). In a by-election in 1997 in the town of Vitrolles, another Marseille suburb with high unemployment, a fourth National Front mayor took power — Catherine Mégret, the wife of Bruno, who was barred from standing himself because of financial irregularities in an earlier campaign.

The behaviour of the four Front mayors gives an inkling of what a Le Pen presidency might do, bearing in mind that local authorities' powers are very restricted by comparison. In the ancient Roman city of Orange, Jacques Bompard at once cut the civic budget by 15 million francs and got rid of what he called 'useless staff'.[4] His savings were achieved by removing subsidies from cultural bodies and from voluntary organisations that helped immigrants and others on the fringes of society. He expelled African traders from the outdoor market, and sent the city police out on night patrols. The head of the municipal library was sacked, and books by African and other foreign writers were removed — replaced with works by National Front leaders and books examining the international Jewish-Masonic conspiracy. *Le Monde* ran a headline saying 'Orange under the reign of hatred'. The mayor of Toulon's assault on the arts (including the jailing of a rap group for insulting the police) caused hundreds of eminent film-makers, writers and artists to march through the city's streets in protest — only to be mocked by the mayor's wife, who stood on a balcony at city hall with a glass of

118

champagne in her hand, blowing them kisses. In Vitrolles, Mme Mégret pulled no punches. She sacked eighty staff, cut aid to welfare bodies by 50 per cent, dismissed a cinema manageress for showing a film about homosexuals, and more than trebled the strength of the town's police force, stationing most of them in immigrant housing estates. She even wanted to offer couples with French citizenship a cash grant for every child, but was ruled out of order by the courts. A court also gave her a three-month suspended sentence and a 50,000 franc fine for 'complicity in public provocation towards racial hatred' after she made a public speech condemning immigrants. Streets which the previous socialist council in Vitrolles had named after figures such as Nelson Mandela or Olof Palme were renamed: Avenue Salvador Allende, for example, was named after Jean-Pierre Stirbois, the National Front xenophobe who had scored its first major success in Dreux.

Bruno Mégret's surrogate victory in Vitrolles lent added piquancy both to the National Assembly elections, called for June 1997, and to the struggle for power within the National Front. Mégret was evidently the real power behind his wife's throne, and stood a good chance of using his Vitrolles base to win a seat in the national parliament. It may have been for this reason that Le Pen decided against standing himself in the elections — for fear of being sidelined if his second-in-command did better than him. At any rate, Le Pen began to manoeuvre against Mégret, appointing another leading light, Bruno Gollnisch, as the Front's secretary general. Then, when Le Pen found himself unable to head the party's list for the June 1999 European Parliament elections (being barred because of his conviction for assault), he suggested the position should go, not to Mégret, but to his wife, Jany. (Wives have often been deemed more reliable deputies than potentially rival politicians in this personality-driven party, and children, too: Le Pen's daughter Marine stood as a leading candidate in Lens in 2002, and appears to be being groomed as his successor, turning the National Front into a political dynasty.)

After a series of party meetings marked by increasing acrimony, Mégret precipitated a split by holding a special congress of his supporters in Marignane in January 1999. The new breakaway *Mouvement national républicain* came into being, led by Mégret, which to date has never proved as attractive to voters as the Front.

The division of the far-right vote almost certainly meant that Le Pen's success in the 2002 presidential election could have been even greater: Mégret took 2.34 per cent of the vote. Added to Le Pen's 16.86, it gives a total of 19.2 per cent — almost one voter in five. That proved to be the far right's zenith, however. The second round of the election was dominated by an intense media campaign persuading all voters, of left and right, to rally round President Chirac and demonstrate their contempt for Le Pen. One newspaper encouraged socialists to put clothes pegs on their noses or gloves on their hands as they took the unpleasant step of casting their ballots for Chirac. The two-round French system is said to encourage people to vote with their hearts in the first round but with their heads in the second, and so, having registered a massive protest against the Establishment in round one (including a 28 per cent abstention rate plus the 19.2 per cent for Le Pen/Mégret), they came out in force in the second to ensure there was no chance that an extremist would enter the Elysée Palace. Le Pen's vote increased slightly in real terms to 5,525,032 votes — 53,293 more than voted for the two far-right candidates in the first round — but because there was a much higher turnout (79 per cent) his share of the vote dropped from 19.2 to 17.79 per cent.

In the subsequent parliamentary elections in June, support continued to trickle away. In round one, Front candidates scored less than 12 per cent nationwide. To qualify for the second round a candidate must come first or second or win the votes of at least 12.5 per cent of *registered* voters; only 37 Front candidates did so, and none came first in the second round to win a seat in the National Assembly.

What the future would hold was unclear. It looked as though Le Pen himself was destined because of his age, if nothing else, to take more of a back seat after 2002. The reaction to the presidential vote — condemnation abroad,

horror throughout France, and a massive swing in the parliamentary elections to the *centre*-right — implied that for
the moment, at least, Le Pen, Mégret and their cohorts
would be obliged to rethink their strategies or perhaps
accept that they were unlikely ever to do better than this.

✳

A map published in *L'Express* after the first round of the
2002 presidential election illustrated the 'browning' of
France since the previous contest of 1995. Areas coloured
dark brown showed where the far-right had won at least 20
per cent of the vote. In 1995 there were just a few patches,
mainly along the Mediterranean coast from the Rhone
estuary to the Italian border, and in the north-eastern
shoulder of France — Alsace and part of Lorraine. In 2002
the brown plague had advanced to cover the entire north-
eastern third of the country, plus all regions along the
coast from Spain to Italy. The *département* of Vaucluse,
which contains the towns of Avignon and Orange, was the
champion, with 29.7 per cent. Close on its heels were the
resorts and port-cities of the French Riviera, and the wine-
growing provinces of Alsace and Moselle. The farming folk
of Corrèze, just east of the Dordogne, flew the ant-fascist
flag — but even there the combined vote for Le Pen and
Mégret, though the lowest in the country, was 10.1 per
cent.

So why do so many French people vote for the far right? With its anti-foreigner bias, one might expect the National Front to do best in areas with large immigrant communities, and generally that is true: cities such as Marseille and Toulon do indeed have many people of North African origin. But close analysis of voting patterns suggests a more complex picture. Support for the National Front is often higher in rural areas *near* cities with many immigrants than in those neighbourhoods themselves. Studies have found that racist attitudes (and hence support for the National Front) are often higher in wards with tiny ethnic minorities, and lower in districts where Maghrebis and 'poor whites' rub shoulders. As John Ardagh writes: 'In these and other suburbs, there may well be scuffles between rival youth gangs: but the adults mostly tolerate each other, because they have got to know and have de-demonised each other. The conclusion is ringingly clear: anti-immigrant hatred in France is above all a matter of ignorance and fear of the unknown.'[5] Ignorance extends also to the richer classes of Neuilly, a smart suburb of Paris, and the 16th *arrondissement* of the capital itself, where 16-17 per cent of voters have supported Le Pen. Surveys show an increasing number of women and young people voting for the National Front, and also growing support among the working classes and disillusioned left-wingers, attracted perhaps by the 'caring' policies dubbed *gaucho-lepénisme* or 'left-wing Lepenism'.

A ballot cast for the National Front means different things to different people. For some it is a protest vote — for policies simply unavailable from mainstream parties. This was particularly the case in 2002, after five years of 'cohabitation' between a right-wing president and a socialist prime minister, Lionel Jospin, who between them were pursuing the kind of mushy coalition policies that also produced a backlash, in the form of votes for the far-right, in Austria and Holland. Chirac and Jospin had become the Tweedledee and Tweedledum of French politics, always seen together at European summits (where other countries made do with just one leader!) and symbolising the immobility of a system that offered few radical choices, just a giant, unimaginative, two-headed monster, shifting its weight a little from foot to foot over the years. Their election manifestoes were so similar that only really committed election-followers could spot much difference. Both men, picking up Le Pen's refrain, pledged to be tough on crime — but then, they had already had five years to do something about that, so why believe them now? No Le Pen supporters, surely, believed he could become president, but a vote for him would at least register a protest against the incumbent duo and shock the Establishment — and it certainly did.

Other factors are also at play. Le Pen appeals on an emotional level to those concerned by high unemployment, crime or racial tension, but also intellectually to voters persuaded by straight political arguments — on the effect of globalisation on French jobs, for example, or the ceding of French sovereignty to the European Union. His pledges to reduce taxes appeal to those who believe previous governments of centre-left and centre-right have consistently overspent to fund a lavish socialistic welfare state. And — as in other countries where extreme, 'outsider' politicians have done well — he offers the electorate a 'clean pair of hands' to wipe out the alleged corruption of the Establishment parties. In 2002, President Chirac was an easy target: allegations of sleaze dripped from every newspaper page, yet a court had ruled that he could not even be questioned about them while he remained in office. The most serious claims referred to his long service as mayor of Paris in the eighties and early nineties, when his RPR party was alleged to have gained millions of francs in kickbacks for public housing contracts. Testimonies from those involved abounded. One property developer, Jean-Claude Mery, described in a video released only after his death how he had handed a case containing 5 million francs to one of Chirac's aides in order to win a housing contract. The money went into the party's coffers. A series of corruption enquiries brought forth allegations suggesting that Chirac gave fake jobs to his cronies, rigged elections, paid for spurious foreign journeys for his family and friends, and fiddled expenses on a mammoth scale. For decades French politics had been beset by such scandals. Le Pen, by contrast, was Mr Clean, and promised to bring the corrupt to book.

And then there is that other reason for voting for Le Pen — one that most French people would prefer to deny: anti-Semitism. Certainly anti-Arab, anti-Muslim sentiment is more dominant these days both in the French public at large and in National Front diatribes: Le Pen's xenophobia is most obviously directed against immigrants from North Africa. But his regular digs at Jews and Jewish influence betray a deep-seated obsession. He baited the popular health minister of the seventies, Simone Veil, for her Jewishness: 'When I speak of genocide, I always say that in any case they missed old woman Veil.' He accused Chirac of being in the pay of Jewish organisations. He dismissed the trial of Maurice Papon, for his role in the deportation of Jews to the Nazi death camps, as an example of 'Judeo-centrism' by which 'history must necessarily order itself by events which affect the Jewish community'.

Such comments may strike a chord in a society with a long history of anti-Semitism and the largest Jewish community — 600,000 — in Western Europe. Acts of violence against Jews are thankfully infrequent, notwithstanding the desecration of a Jewish cemetery in Carpentras in 1990 by skinheads later identified as members of a neo-Nazi group. Nothing to do with me, Le Pen protested. But his own constant verbal vilification scarcely contributes to an atmosphere of tolerance.

126

Like many far-right populist politicians in Europe, Le Pen has not needed to gain formal power at national level in order to have many of his views accepted and policies introduced, in one form or another. Even before he established the National Front as France's third political force, he got used to hearing mainstream politicians on the left and right parroting his views. As far back as 1976 Jacques Chirac, then prime minister under President Valérie Giscard d'Estaing, remarked: 'A country which has 900,000 unemployed but more than two million immigrant workers is not a country in which the problem of jobs is insoluble.'[6] This is not to say that Chirac adopted the notion of reducing unemployment by kicking out foreigners from Le Pen; on the contrary, it shows that the idea was current even before the National Front made it one of its central policies.

Successive French governments have toughened the country's immigration laws in response to a public mood that both fed into and was fanned by the National Front. Giscard d'Estaing virtually banned immigrant labour from outside the European Community, and offered 10,000 francs to any foreign workers who agreed to go home. Mitterrand, true to his socialist and anti-racist credentials, extended full welfare rights to immigrants and made family reunification easier, but at the same time thousands of illegal immigrants were deported, and new discriminatory checks were imposed at the borders. When a centre-right government returned, for a period of cohabitation with Mitterrand in 1993-95, the new immigration minister, Charles Pasqua, demanded 'zero illegal immigration': he imposed tougher police checks, and drastically restricted the issuing of visas and residence permits, and family reunification. Another law deprived children born in France to immigrant parents of the automatic right to citizenship. After 1995, with the right-wing Chirac as president and a government to match, and successes for the National Front at local level demonstrating the public mood, xenophobic policies took off. A parliamentary committee proposed depriving immigrants without valid papers of health care, and suggested that people who put them up should be listed by the police. In 1996 Chirac adopted heavy-handed police tactics to evict a group of three hundred African immigrants who had taken refuge in the Church of St Bernard in Paris, causing indignation in left-wing circles — though nothing compared to the outcry provoked by a bill tabled a few months later which required citizens to report the arrival and departure of foreigners staying in their homes. Intellectuals and cultural celebrities protested vehemently at what they described as a throwback to the Nazi period, saying they would never comply, and hoped to be prosecuted. The measure was dropped when Lionel Jospin's socialist government came to power in 1997. He also reinstated the automatic right to citizenship for any child born in France. But other anti-immigration measures introduced by the right remained in place.

As he surveyed the disarray on the battlefield following his 2002 presidential bid, Le Pen had the satisfaction of knowing that even if his dream of becoming president was never going to come true, his vision — at least parts of it — was already a reality. Immigration was the number one issue not just in France but around Europe. The re-elected Chirac declared it a priority. The insinuation that most crimes were committed by immigrants had gained such currency that one rarely heard the proposition gainsaid.

Here, as in Europe as a whole, governments have decided that the way to deal with the electoral challenge from the extreme right is not to oppose or expose them, not to hold their ideas up to ridicule or demonstrate their inhumanity or stupidity, but to copy them, in the hope of winning over their voters. As a result, the politics of populism are endowed with credibility, legitimacy and respectability. It may even encourage more people to vote for them, on the principle: why choose a government that only reluctantly adopts policies I like, and waters them down and prevaricates, when I can vote for the real thing?

Notes

1 *Le Monde*, 15 July and 23 April 2002.

2 www.lepen.tv/3/projet/htm.

3 Edward G. Declair, *Politics on the Fringe*, Duke University Press 1999, p. 42.

4 John Ardagh, *France in the New Century*, London: Penguin, 2000, p. 249.

5 *Ibid.*, p. 247.

6 Quoted by Paul Hainsworth, *op. cit.*, p. 26.

5.

Italy's Tainted Triumvirate

If any country mans the drawbridge of Europe, facing the legendary tide of refugees arriving from Asia and Africa, it is Italy. Its 5,000-mile coastline is impossible to police efficiently, and is a magnet for illegal landings of ships carrying immigrants. In the early nineties it was the obvious first safe haven for Albanians who made the quick but perilous dash across the fifty-mile stretch of the Adriatic in speedboats or any rickety vessel that came to hand, to flee the fighting and poverty that followed the collapse of communism in their homeland. Nowadays the migrants are more likely to have paid thousands of dollars to unscrupulous people-traffickers — gangs such as the Snakeheads in the far east — and may have travelled for months over land

and sea, in containers or rusting boats. It is a considerable risk. Even as they enter European waters, their safe arrival is not certain. In November 2001 eight hundred Kurdish passengers were abandoned by the crew on a burning boat off Greece. A year earlier 24 immigrants drowned when the vessel on which they were being smuggled into Europe capsized off the island of Kos. Sometimes the human cargo is forced to abandon ship well short of the coast, and swim or wade ashore. One day in June 2002, before dawn, smugglers forced 43 Kurds at knife point into the water a kilometre from the shore, just south of the Italian town of Otranto; four of them drowned.

In March 2002 a scarcely seaworthy vessel named the *Monica* steamed over the horizon and presented itself to the authorities of Catania, in Sicily, who reluctantly had it towed into port after the crew threatened to throw babies overboard if they refused. The cargo ship was stuffed with people, like a slave ship of old — stubble-faced men, black-clad mothers and pregnant women, dark-eyed little children and babies. They were Kurds, from Iraq, looking for refuge from Saddam Hussein's murderous regime — a regime which had used chemical weapons against some of its Kurdish citizens. Even so, the reaction in Italy was one of outrage, not welcome, with the most unrestrained invective coming from the populist leader of the nationalist Northern League (and minister in the right-wing Italian government), Umberto Bossi. He demanded the appointment of an immigration commissioner with emergency powers, and ranted: 'I am fed up with these crocodile tears over immigrants. It is time for action. If I had my way we would sink these smugglers' ships, blow them out of the water, not just confiscate them.' Whether he wished to blow them up with the immigrants on board was not clear, but even judged by the standards of this demagogue-in-chief of Italy's far right, the words went beyond the pale.

In fact, relatively few refugees actually remain in Italy. Under the Dublin Convention, asylum seekers are supposed to make their applications in the first EU country they enter, but many use Italy as a staging post, passing on quickly to other countries through the passport-free borders of the Schengen system. Italy — with the sixth-largest economy in the world — ranks only 25th in the league of industrialised countries receiving asylum applications. In 2001 it processed only 9,620 cases, compared to 88,000 in Germany and the UK, and 47,000 in France. Illegal immigrants who fail to register at all are, by definition, impossible to count. It is estimated that there are at least 300,000 of them in Italy — but even that number is small compared to Britain or Germany, each of which believes it has around a million.

Nonetheless the right-wing Italian government led by Silvio Berlusconi — which included not just Bossi but also the leader of Italy's 'post-fascist' National Alliance, Gianfranco Fini — launched a crackdown on illegal immigration soon after it was sworn in, in June 2001. It began deporting 30 per cent more asylum seekers than the previous government. A new law passed in 2002 making deportation easier caused a howl of protest by also requiring that all immigrants be fingerprinted. The Catholic left alleged racial discrimination against *'extra-communitari'* or non-EU citizens, but this lessened when it emerged that all Italian citizens and residents would have their fingerprints on new photo identity cards being phased in over the next two years.

The government was active in pushing the European Union towards new, tougher rules. It hosted a meeting of EU foreign ministers in 2002 (even though Spain was formally president of the Union at the time) to present a feasibility study on the joint policing of Europe's borders.

For all that, it was less immigration that helped the far right to prosper than a variety of unique Italian factors. One was the lingering influence of fascism: elements of Mussolini's pre-war party had created the Italian Social Movement, which was rebranded as the *Alleanza Nationale* (National Alliance) by its leader, Fini, in 1994. Describing fascism as an exceptional historical period that could not be repeated, Fini preferred to call his party 'post-fascist' rather than 'neo-fascist', and continually stressed his adherence to the political mainstream; but doubts lingered about the sincerity of his conversion — and even more so of others in his party, many of whom continued to believe that 'many positive things were done' under Mussolini up until 1938 when he threw in his lot with Hitler. The party also never gave up its territorial claims on land 'lost' to Yugoslavia after the War. It twice entered a government led by Silvio Berlusconi — for a brief period in 1994 and again from June 2001.

Second was the spectre of separatism, which came in the controversial form of Umberto Bossi's *Lega Nord* — the Northern League for the Independence of Padania, to give it its full name (Padania being the northern part of Italy which Bossi 'declared' an independent republic in September 1996). As well as secession for the north — not in itself necessarily a policy associated with the far right — Bossi embraced many of the traditional traits of Europe's Le Pens and Haiders. He supported the crackdown on immigration, described the EU, with its ever deepening integration, as 'the Soviet Union of the West', and made abusive comments about homosexuals.

The third factor was the corruption and political imbroglio in which Italy found itself in the early nineties — a situation which Fini, Bossi and above all Berlusconi were able to exploit. Berlusconi does not fit entirely into any definition of 'far right', indeed, some would describe him as 'centre right'. But if his economic policies were no more extreme than those practised in post-Thatcher Britain, his drive to monopolise the mass media and refusal to separate his business interests from politics were deeply worrying. It was hard to know who to fear most in Italy's hard right triumvirate: the rabble-rousing Bossi because of his xenophobia, the television smoothie Fini because no one could be sure he had really jettisoned his fascist roots, or Berlusconi because he was an unscrupulous tycoon with a criminal record and a thirst for power.

*

Italy at the beginning of the nineties was ripe for just about anything. Thanks partly to a pure form of proportional representation which allowed tiny parties to get into parliament and never gave any single party a governing majority, the system produced a succession of unstable governments. Coalitions came and went with great regularity like a shifting kaleidoscope of the same five parties — the Christian Democrats, the Socialists, the Liberals, the Social Democrats and the Republicans — which came to be known as the *pentapartito*. It was the apotheosis of the neither-here-nor-there tradition of coalition-building that would lead people to seek radical alternatives to the mainstream in several European countries.

Behind the scenes, Italian politics was riddled with corruption and prey to secret lobbies — from the notorious P2 Masonic lodge to the Mafia. Every level of government was tainted, from local administrations to prime ministers and party leaders. Briefcases stuffed with used banknotes arrived at town halls and party headquarters as 'political payment' for contracts, favours and deals. Public and even private appointments, as well as the allocation of resources, were in the gift of the political parties. This political division of the spoils of office (*lottizzazzione*) was chronic, for example, inside the state broadcaster, RAI, where it extended from top management right down to radio engineers. A referendum on 9 June 1991, which most politicians and the media advised voters to ignore, in fact produced a large turnout and a 95.6 per cent vote in favour of reforming the election system.

The public was ready for bigger changes, but popular disgust with the corrupt system made little difference until the watershed year of 1992, when investigating magistrates in Milan began uncovering a spectacular bribery network. It began in February after a senior socialist politician in the city was arrested — as he desperately tried to flush 30 million lire just received in bribes down the lavatory — and decided to tell magistrates all he knew. The city was dubbed 'Bribesville' (*Tangentopoli*). It led to the so-called 'Clean Hands' operation, which raged like a hurricane through the political, business and administrative elite. Thousands of prominent figures would be arrested and a few imprisoned.

The first sign that the people's patience had finally run out came in the general election of April 1992, when the *pentapartito* was snubbed, receiving less than half of the votes cast. The press called it an 'earthquake'. Over the next year or so, as the Clean Hands investigation widened far beyond Milan and snared hundreds of members of parliament as well as local politicians, managers, civil servants and top executives, almost the entire Establishment and existing political parties were swept away. The Communist Party — which had been the most influential in western Europe — had already imploded in 1991, following the collapse of communism in the Soviet bloc and an admission that its ideas were now bankrupt. Now the others followed it into oblivion. The five parties which had governed Italy in various combinations since the War either fell apart, changed their name, or lost their identity — and with it their influence, their funding, their members and their voters. The Christian Democrats became the *Popolari* or 'People's Party' and faded away. The total disintegration of the socialist party was described by one observer as a tragedy for Italian democracy: 'The leadership of Bettino Craxi, initially welcomed by many for its vigour, youth and modernism, transformed the party beyond recognition, sucking nearly all and sundry into a vortex of corrupt and authoritarian relations.'[1] Craxi himself fled to Tunisia to escape arrest and was later found guilty in absentia on multiple corruption charges. The Christian Democrat prime minister, Giulio Andreotti, was charged with selling political favours to the Mafia and with complicity in the murder of a journalist in 1979 (he was later acquitted). As if to add to the political mayhem, the Mafia staged a series of terrifying bomb attacks — targeted with great precision against magistrates, journalists and even cultural targets such as the church of San Giorgio in Velabro in the centre of old Rome — as a warning to anyone who dared to challenge it.

If ever there was a political vacuum waiting to be filled, if ever a society was crying out for a strong hand to restore order, this was it. The stage was set for the rebirth of Italian politics, and the far right was ready to step into the limelight.

Umberto Bossi's plans were most advanced. He had founded his Northern League in November 1989, bringing together several regional separatist movements. The party was the big winner in the 1992 election, taking 8.7 per cent of the nationwide vote, but all of that, naturally, in the north — including 25 per cent in Lombardy. Any doubts about whether Bossi should be included under the rubric of 'far right' may be dispelled by quoting from his speech to the League's first national congress: '[Assimilation] could not apply to black immigrants, for whom integration is not foreseeable even at the distance of many centuries. With them the classic mechanisms of social integration, which are marriage and children, do not function, with the result that it would be impossible to build an ethnic link without generating grave racial tensions within society.' And, from an interview given in 1990: 'I have expelled at most six people from the party. Among them was a lad who was trustworthy and with the right values, but he was homosexual. How many of the major parties have self-declared homosexuals, i.e. effeminate weaklings, in key posts?'[2]

No description of Bossi ever appears without reference to his badly tailored suits and scruffy appearance, but that is the least of it. He may have looked a rough-and-ready politician, but he was a charismatic speaker with a flair for crude, even foul-mouthed, populist talk. He could whip up emotions with his diatribes against the south. His xenophobia extended not just to blacks but to merely swarthy southern Italians who had migrated north in search of work. Crowds would take an oath of loyalty, and pledge not to tolerate the existence of Italy but to fight for a free Padania. At his rallies you could buy Padanian banknotes, passports and even blood-donor certificates — all inscribed with Bossi's likeness and a green three-pointed plant emblem.[3]

The rationale behind the League's separatism was more economic than ethnic: Bossi believed the hard-working, entrepreneurial north could thrive better without the more backward, 'lazy' south of Italy. But he soon showed that he was interested in much more than mere independence for Padania. In 1993 he began to present his movement as a potential national force, arguing for a new devolved, federalist form of government.

To the south, the second member of the coming triumvirate, Gianfranco Fini, was also surveying the chaos of 1992 and plotting his future. Fini had been leader of the Italian Social Movement (MSI), the post-war successor to Mussolini's Fascist Party, since 1987, apart from a short break in 1990-91. Born in 1952, he was the most modern of Italian politicians, adept on television, eloquent, smartly dressed, cool-headed. Against the backdrop of almost universal political corruption and confusion, he was able to appear both 'clean' and focused. Fini's first opportunity to capitalise on the political void came in municipal elections in late 1993, when he stood for the post of mayor of Rome — while the party's candidate in Naples was Mussolini's granddaughter, Alessandra. Neither won, but their shares of the vote — 47 and 43 per cent respectively — was early evidence of a shift in Italian opinion. In Rome the MSI became the biggest single party — a remarkable turnaround for a party that a few years earlier had seemed to be heading for extinction.

For the general election of 1994 Fini took the first step towards revamping the MSI, to give it the appearance of a mainstream, moderate-right force, concentrating on tackling popular issues such as high taxes and illegal immigration. At a party conference in January he announced that the MSI would contest the election under the auspices of (and as the leading member of) a right-wing umbrella group, the National Alliance — a name it would take for itself a year later. But was Fini's declared commitment to work within the democratic system more than a ploy to make his party electable? One only needed to look inside the party's branch headquarters to see that old-fashioned fascism was still very much alive. In May 1994 a reporter for *La Repubblica* described the Nomentano party section in Rome, of which Fini was a member, as follows: 'Mussolini reigns like a monarch in every room. His portrait, either in profile or full-face, with or without helmet, is to be found on every wall and behind the desks of the sections' officers.'[4] The party celebrated its seventieth anniversary in October 1992 with a well-attended demonstration in Rome 'complete with fascist hymns and Roman salutes.'[5] And a survey of attitudes among the party's delegates to an MSI conference in 1990 found that 94 per cent agreed with the statement that 'the United States is an imperialist power', 90 per cent that 'the family is the pillar of society', 79 per cent that 'the reproduction habits of immigrants threaten our national identity', and 74 per cent that 'discipline is the basis of the social order'. Some 64 per cent declared themselves to be anti-Zionist, 25 per cent anti-Semitic, and 32 per cent regarded armed struggle as an acceptable way of securing political change.[6]

Neither Fini nor Bossi would have made it into national government were it not for their alliance with

Silvio Berlusconi. The media magnate, possibly Italy's richest man, had almost total dominance of Italy's national commercial television networks and business interests stretching from his Fininvest empire to ownership of the AC Milan football club. Unlike most of his friends in high places, he was not — at this stage — under investigation for corruption. In 1993 he spotted the chance to break into politics. In November he founded a national party which he named, with all the guile of a modern PR man, after a football supporters' chant: 'Forza Italia' — 'Go, Italy!' When elections were announced in January 1994 Berlusconi reacted with astounding speed to launch his political infant into the campaign, and within days formed alliances with Fini and Bossi. In the north he created 'The Pole of Liberty' with the Northern League, and in the rest of the country, where Bossi's party was not standing, he formed 'The Pole of Good Government' with the National Alliance. For such a political 'novice' it was a masterstroke, maximising his nationwide appeal even though his two partners had no time for each other and were poles apart politically, representing quite different aspects of far-right politics: Bossi's racism and homophobia were not part of Fini's 'post'-fascism; Bossi wanted to break up the Italian state while Fini was nationalistically committed to it; Bossi was a free-marketeer, while Fini wanted a strong centralised and interventionist state.

Berlusconi insisted his own party was a centrist, Catholic-inspired one. Economically, he was not unlike Mrs Thatcher or even Tony Blair in Britain, advocating free enterprise, low taxes, and the use of the private sector to provide more efficient public services. In his first public speech, in Rome in February 1994, he listed Forza Italia's principles as 'belief in freedom, the person, the family, enterprise, Italian tradition, Christian tradition and love for weaker people — the sick, the young, the old and the under-privileged'.[7] But by aligning himself with Fini and Bossi he provided them with a leg-up into government and legitimised their more extreme ideas by presenting them as part of the mainstream.

After a campaign unsurprisingly skewed by Berlusconi's media empire, and under a reformed voting system which combined a proportional element with a first-past-the-post element, the right-wing coalition gained 366 of the 630 seats in parliament. Forza Italia was the biggest single party, with 21 per cent of the vote, just ahead of the renamed socialists. Fini's National Alliance became the country's third party, with 13.5 per cent, and Bossi's Northern League won 8.4 per cent — but 118 seats, making it the biggest faction. Fini's party gained five ministerial posts in Berlusconi's new government, while the Northern League took charge of the interior ministry.

There was considerable unease abroad at the far right's success, which increased further when 200 black-shirted and skinhead supporters paraded in Vicenza to celebrate, and Fini described Mussolini as 'the greatest statesman of the century'. The National Alliance tabled a proposal in parliament to remove the ban that had prevented a revival of the Fascist Party since the War, and Fini spoke in terms that suggested his commitment to democracy was paper-thin: 'There are periods in which liberty is not the most important value. Fascism suppressed liberty of association for the benefit of social progress.'[8] He asserted that until 1938, when Mussolini introduced Nazi-style racial laws against Italy's Jews, 'it was very difficult to judge fascism in a negative way.'[9] Other members of his party proposed redrawing the country's border with the former Yugoslavia to reincorporate land that had belonged to Mussolini's Italy, and revived a dispute over Italian property claims in neigh-bouring Slovenia — a dispute that appeared to lie behind the Berlusconi government's vetoing of Slovenia's application to join the European Union. Italy's ambiguous role in the former Yugoslavia, and in particular its raising of territorial claims, meant that it was excluded from the international Contact Group set up in 1994 to mediate in the Bosnian conflict.

Now, during the election campaign, Berlusconi had criticised the 'red-robed' inquisitors of the Clean Hands investigation, and one of the first things he did as prime minister was to pass a decree which effectively put an end to the anti-corruption campaign which had done so much to help bring him to power. The outcry — led by the Milan investigators, who were keen to continue with their inquiries — was so immense that Berlusconi had to backtrack. It did not take a genius to work out why the media mogul was so keen to muzzle the magistrates. In November, while he was presiding over a G7 meeting in Naples, Berlusconi was handed notification that he was under investigation by the Clean Hands squad in connection with inquiries into systematic bribing of the tax police. Other corruption charges soon followed, and though they were hotly denied by Berlusconi, it spelt the end of his government after just seven months.

Umberto Bossi, who in any case had been a disruptive presence, and was angry that his goal of a federal Italy had been pushed aside, withdrew his support. Berlusconi resigned on 22 December 1994. Italy's first flirtation with the far right was over.

After a year of government by 'technocrats', fresh elections in 1996 brought Romano Prodi's centre-left 'Olive Tree' coalition to power. In opposition for the next six years, the far right would have a chance to rethink and regroup — beginning with Gianfranco Fini's formal launch of the National Alliance in January 1995 as the successor to the Italian Social Movement. This was yet another attempt by him to convince the public, and observers abroad, of his break with fascism, and in this he was aided by the refusal of a hardline faction, led by Pino Rauti, to join the new party. Opinion polls in early 1996 showed Fini to be the country's most popular politician — and with 15.7 per cent in the election his National Alliance cemented its position as Italy's third largest party. In 1998 Fini held yet another conference to 'relaunch' the Alliance as 'a modern, open, right-wing party'. His feud with Bossi continued unabated. The latter stepped up his secessionist drive for Padania after the Northern League increased its vote to 10.1 per cent in the 1996 election, becoming the largest party in the North. A 'Padanian Liberation Committee' was established, and in September three days of 'independence celebrations' were held. Bossi flew to the source of the River Po (after which Padania is named), filled a test tube with its water and later, after a triumphal progress along the waterway in a motorised catamaran, he emptied it into the lagoon in Venice. Here, he proclaimed Padania's 'independence' at a rally of about 15,000 supporters. The shine was taken off this theatrical event, however, by a counter-demonstration the same day in Milan, organised by Fini in support of Italian unity — which attracted 150,000 people.

*

The next chance for Berlusconi to make a comeback was in the elections of 2001. But by now he was more controversial than ever, having been found guilty in first-level courts on charges of illegally financing a political party, false accounting, and four charges of corruption, including bribing financial police. (He remained at large only under a 'statute of limitations' which extinguishes a crime after the lapse of time allowed for a case to be heard at all three levels of Italian justice.) As *The Economist* pointed out, 'In any self-respecting democracy it would be unthinkable that the man assumed to be on the verge of being elected prime minister would recently have come under investigation for, among other things, money-laundering, complicity in murder, connections with the Mafia, tax evasion and the bribing of politicians, judges and the tax police.'[10] The remarks came in a highly unusual and blatant attempt by the news magazine to influence Italy's election. 'Why Silvio Berlusconi is unfit to lead Italy,' said the front cover, which was backed up with a detailed investigation inside.

The magazine gave details from ongoing trials and investigations. It alleged he had used a 75-year-old stroke victim as a front in a multi-billion lire money laundering operation. It spoke of a secret offshore empire, of a trail of money from Berlusconi to a judge with links to the Mafia, and of much more besides. Apart from alleged crimes, the magazine emphasised the conflict of interests between Berlusconi's business and political activities. 'When he entered politics,' it wrote, 'he gave up the directorships of all his Fininvest companies, except AC Milan... However, he remains the controlling shareholder, and one or both of his grown-up children sit on the board of each of the main companies in the empire... Between them, Mr Berlusconi's three TV networks (Canale 5, Italia 1 and Retequattro) have a 43 per cent share of the national audience and over 60 per cent of total TV advertising sales... He has a controlling stake in another quoted company, Mondadori, which is Italy's largest publishing group. Mondadori's books division has almost 30 per cent of the domestic market; its magazine division, with around 50 titles, 38 per cent. The Berlusconi family also owns one of Italy's leading national newspapers, *Il Giornale...*' Sadly, *The Economist* was forced to admit, much of this was known in Italy, 'yet most Italians seem untroubled'.

'Almost perversely supportive' would have been nearer the mark. In the May 2001 elections Berlusconi's Forza Italia surged ahead to become the largest party in the country, with 29.4 per cent of the proportional vote. This time his allies suffered — Bossi's Northern League fell from 10.1 to just 4 per cent, Fini's National Alliance from 15.7 to 12 per cent. Nonetheless Bossi himself entered the cabinet, as minister for reforms and devolution, while Fini became deputy prime minister. Fini later also received the honour of representing Italy on the Convention on the Future of Europe, the body chaired by former French president Giscard-d'Estaing to elaborate EU reforms.

The jury is out on this second Berlusconi administration, but it has already proved controversial. Renato Ruggiero, the experienced and distinguished foreign minister, resigned

149

in protest at his government's anti-European stance. Italy's EU partners were already concerned by Berlusconi's attitudes. He had tried to stop the adoption of an EU-wide arrest warrant as part of the community's response to the September 11th attacks. Italy was the only country not to stage celebrations for the launch of the single currency. And Berlusconi had exposed the EU summit in the Brussels suburb of Laeken in December 2001 to ridicule with his puerile squabbling over where to site a new EU food safety authority. He wanted it to be based in Parma, the French wanted it in Lille and the Finns put forward Helsinki. 'Pah!' Berlusconi spluttered. 'What do the Finns know about good food? They don't even know what *prosciutto* is!'

In the domestic arena, the prime minister consolidated his control of Italian television by securing a more right-wing governing board on the state broadcaster, RAI. Critics said that, together with his commercial stations, he now controlled 90 per cent of the Italian television market. Concerns deepened in June 2002 when two political shows, hosted by critics of Berlusconi, were dropped. Significantly, the Italian president, Carlo Azeglio Ciampi, called for pluralism and impartiality to be upheld in the nation's media.

The idea of a man combining his near-monopoly of the media with the prime-ministership of his country would be hard to imagine in any other democracy. As Giovanni Sartori, a professor of constitutional law, put it: 'The only solution is, he should be obliged to sell — if he wants to remain prime minister of course. He can choose to hold his empire, to be a [media magnate like Rupert] Murdoch, and if so not to be a prime minister. In England I don't think Murdoch would be acceptable as prime minister. And it is the same here in Italy.'

But Berlusconi was looking to increase his powers. In July he indicated that he would like the Italian presidency to be turned into a more powerful, French-style post — and that he would like the job. Such a turn of events would, of course, make it even harder to bring Berlusconi to court for his alleged misdemeanours. In the meantime, he has had to make do with changing the law: by effectively decriminalising false accounting, three of the cases hanging over him were expected to evaporate.

September 11th breathed new life into the xenophobia of Berlsuconi's Northern League partners, and imbued it with an explicit anti-Islamic tinge. A month after the attacks one member of the party named Speroni, who served as undersecretary in Umberto Bossi's Ministry of Reforms, called on the government to stop issuing entry visas to Muslims as a preventive measure in a war situation. He was supported by Bossi, who took the chance to emphasise his party's populist credentials: 'There is a war going on; if the situation gets worse, if we risk a disaster, if we risk dying of Ebola, it is wise to stop new Muslim immigrants from entering. Speroni speaks the people's language; the people think the same way. Fortunately the Northern League speaks the people's language and not the language of politicians.' At a demonstration in Riva del Garda (Trento), League activists shouted 'Self-defence from Islam' and 'Padanialand is Christian land'. The mayor of Varese, also a League member, had surveillance cameras installed outside the local mosque 'as a goodwill measure to residents, who are disturbed by the Muslim presence', while his colleague in Treviso had a warehouse being used as a mosque closed down.[11]

Other members of the governing coalition distanced themselves from the blatantly Islamophobic statements of the Northern League, but Berlusconi himself echoed them. While visiting Berlin he caused a furore by remarking that Western culture was 'superior' to Muslim culture (he later claimed his words had been taken out of context). His policies, too, were heavily influenced by the League, and by the National Alliance. Berlusconi launched a major crackdown on crime and illegal immigration. In one operation a thousand foreigners were summarily expelled for being in the country without papers, and a further three hundred were arrested on charges of running prostitution and drug rackets. In a second operation in May 2002, code-named 'High Impact', more than 240 people were arrested and hundreds of illegal immigrants detained pending deportation. In June a new draconian immigration law, known as the 'Bossi-Fini' law after its creators, was condemned by one opposition politician as 'unjust, fascist, disgusting, enslaving and racist'. It meant that non-EU foreigners would only be able to live in Italy if they had arranged work before entering, and would receive a residence permit only for the duration of their contracts, up to a maximum of two years. The law also made family reunions more difficult, obliged foreigners to provide fingerprints for identification purposes, and said that any immigrants who returned after being expelled would be treated as criminals.

At another time, perhaps, the legislation would have come in for condemnation around Europe — if Austria had proposed it, for instance, after the Freedom Party joined the government. But things had changed. By the summer of 2002 European governments were vying with each other to produce the harshest anti-immigration laws. Behind the scenes, many of Berlusconi's European colleagues were appalled by his megalomaniac and anti-democratic tendencies, but few spoke out. Only Chancellor Schröder of Germany dared to class Berlusconi along with Europe's hard-right populists. 'We cannot allow Europe to fall into the hands of people like Berlusconi, Haider or Le Pen,' he wrote for a newsletter published by Looking to the Right, an organisation which examines far-right activity in Europe.

Or rather, he didn't quite dare. He did write that, but had the sentence excised from his article before publication.

Notes

1 Paul Ginsborg, *Italy and its Discontents*, London: Allen Lane, 2001, p. 282.

2 Both quotations from Ginsborg, *op. cit.*, p. 176 and p. 413.

3 Nicholas Fraser, *The Voice of Modern Hatred*, London: Picador, 2000, p. 260.

4 A. Longo, 'La svolta di Fini si ferma in sezione', *La Repubblica*, 8 May 1994, quoted in Ginsborg, *op. cit.*, p. 447.

5 Ginsborg, *op. cit.*, p. 288.

6 P. Ignazi, *Postfascisti?*, Bologna, 1994, pp.80-89; quoted in Ginsborg, *op. cit.*, p. 448, and in Tom Gallacher, 'The Italian Far Right in the 1990s', in Hainsworth (ed.), *op.cit.*, p. 70.

7 Forza Italia website.

8 *La Stampa*, 3 June 1994.

[9] Gallacher, *op. cit.*, p.76.

[10] *The Economist*, 26 April 2001.

[11] European Monitoring Centre on Racism and Xenophobia, 'Anti-Islamic Reactions in the EU after the Terrorist Attacks against the USA: Italy'.

6.

Holland's Dead Souls

It has never been challenged, but I find it hard to believe that voting in the Dutch general election on 15 May 2002 was legal. The electronic system used did not just allow people to vote for a dead candidate: it seemed almost to encourage it. Let me explain.

Pim Fortuyn, the flamboyant, gay, anti-immigrant politician, whose dramatic rise to prominence in the first months of the year had shocked the Netherlands and the rest of Europe, was assassinated just nine days before polling day. His recently created party, known as the Pim Fortuyn List, consisted of largely unknown men and women, political novices. Had their names appeared singly on ballot papers — even with their party's name attached — it is unlikely that they would have received many votes. Pim Fortuyn *was* his party: he dominated it with his personality, his charisma and his politics, while the other candidates meant nothing to the vast majority of Dutch voters.

But what did voters find when they entered the polling stations? In most of them, voting was done electronically, at a kind of console covered with buttons for all the candidates, arranged vertically in columns under their party's name. You voted by pressing one button: a vote for any particular candidate counted as a vote for his or her party — and at the end of the day each party's votes were counted, and seats in parliament distributed among them proportionally. The top button in the column marked *Lijst Pim Fortuyn* (LPF) was for a candidate named 'Pim Fortuyn', even though the man had been dead for more than a week and could not possibly take up a seat in parliament. The overwhelming majority of voters who chose his party pressed the Pim Fortuyn button (he personally received 1,358,942 votes), while only 255,859 voted for all the other candidates on his list. If that top button had not been there — and in a truly democratic vote it should not have been there, since the candidate did not exist — it seems certain that the party would have received a much smaller share of the vote. Thus it was that a vote for a dead soul brought not the larger than life Fortuyn into government, but the lifeless rump of his far-right party.[1]

There was much debate in the days between Fortuyn's murder and the election about whether his party would lose support because of his absence or gain a sympathy vote. The evidence seems to suggest that both things happened, and that the ultimate beneficiary was the centre-right Christian Democratic Party, whose young leader, Jan Peter Balkenende, became prime minister. The share of the vote gained by the Pim Fortuyn List was more or less as opinion polls had predicted — 17 per cent and 26 seats in the 150-member parliament — but I certainly came across many voters at polling stations who said they would have voted for it while its leader was alive, but had decided against voting for a party whose candidates they scarcely knew and whom they did not trust to act sensibly without Fortuyn. This would suggest that the party was deserted by approximately the same number as came to it out of sympathy. Many of the deserters will have gone to the party they considered closest to it politically, namely the Christian Democrats, whose share of the vote — 28 per cent and 43 seats — was considerably higher than opinion polls had suggested.

Whatever the reasons, Holland was launched on to a trajectory far from the known world of twentieth-century Dutch politics. Certainly, the Christian Democrats were no strangers to power, indeed they had had ministers in every government since 1918, apart from an interlude from 1994 to 2002, when the Labour (socialist) Party led the government. But neither Christian Democrats nor Labour had ever governed alone. The Dutch had evolved a system of consensual politics which had come to be regarded as a model of stability and moderation. Tolerance and permissiveness were by-words for Holland, seen in its relaxed attitudes since the sixties to prostitution, drugs, homosexuality, euthanasia, immigration. Elections rarely brought dramatic lurches in policy direction.

But the new government, formed in July by Balkenende with six ministers from his own Christian Democrats, four from the Pim Fortuyn List and three from the Liberals (VVD), embarked on a new course. Not only did it announce plans to restrict the availability of cannabis and to 'review' the recently adopted law on euthanasia, but it decreed an end to Holland's liberal immigration policies — not quite the 'zero immigration' which Fortuyn had called for, but heavily influenced by his views. Indeed, the LPF's Hilbrand Nawijn was appointed minister for asylum and immigration. The post had previously been known as 'integration minister', and had come under the Home Affairs Ministry, whereas Nawijn was to work under the Justice Ministry, a change which critics said brought the issue of integration into the realm of criminal justice. The government said a 'restrictive aliens policy' was necessary and that illegal immigration should be 'fought with vigour'. Dutch asylum procedures were in fact already tougher than might have been expected: one in three applications were rejected within 48 hours. But the new policy would oblige asylum seekers to pay a nearly €7,000 (£4,500) deposit for compulsory Dutch language and citizenship lessons, restrict the ability to bring non-Western family members into the country, and clamp down on businesses employing illegal immigrants. The budget for asylum seeker centres was to be cut by 90 per cent. Other controversial policies included a drastic cut in spending on social welfare, particularly on disability benefit, which one in five of the Dutch labour force received — many of them, it was claimed, fraudulently.

And yet, just how right-wing was Pim Fortuyn? As we shall see, he was no ordinary politician, and certainly no ordinary far-right extremist. Even the word 'populist' may be less appropriate than for Le Pen or Haider, and he himself was incensed if anyone called him a racist. In Fortuyn's case, illiberalism was born of liberalism, far-right coupled with far-left, a paradox through and through. His party, now in power but bereft of its leader, may be more straightforward — and perhaps the more frightening because of it. Even after the election its leaders admitted that they were so lacking in experience that they would have to look beyond the ranks of their MPs for suitable government ministers. Signs of instability were soon evident. The LPF state secretary for emancipation and women's affairs, Philomena Bijlhout, resigned only hours after taking office, after admitting she had lied over her links to the military dictatorship in the South American country of Surinam, where she was born. A month later Mat Herben, the man who replaced Fortuyn as head of the party, resigned, saying he had only taken the job under great pressure. Many commentators said the party lacked credibility, and predicted its collapse.

*

Fortuyn was born in 1948, one of the post-War 'baby boom' generation — a phrase he used in the title of his autobiography, *Babyboomers*. He shared his politics and moral outlook with many of the 'Swinging Sixties' generation, for whom left-wing politics and permissiveness were the order of the day, especially in Holland. *Babyboomers* describes his first sexual encounter as a boy, and the discovery of his homosexuality — the trait that was to become central to the paradox of his unique blend of liberal and reactionary ideas in later years. He became a Marxist, lectured in sociology, and long before he created his political party became a celebrity, as much for his appearance — shaven head, bright ties and matching top-pocket handkerchiefs — as for his outspoken views, which he expressed as a newspaper columnist and television chat-show guest. 'Professor Pim' cultivated a rakish, flamboyant image, with his butler and two lapdogs his constant companions.

It was precisely Fortuyn's belief in the Netherlands' liberal culture and permissive society that led him to his reactionary views on Islam, which he believed was incompatible with Dutch values. In another book, *Against the Islamicisation of our Culture*, he argued that Islam lagged behind western culture and should not be imported; Muslim immigrants should embrace Dutch culture and leave their own values behind. 'Christianity and Judaism have gone through the laundromat of humanism and enlightenment, but that is not the case with Islam,' he said. 'Modern society places an emphasis on individual responsibility, whereas Islam places an emphasis on collective responsibility and the family. We have a separation of state and church. The laws of the country are not subject to the Koran. We have equality of men and women in western society, whereas in Islamic culture women are inferior to men.'[2] He insisted his views were not racist and that he believed in a multi-ethnic society: integrating existing immigrants had to be the priority, however, while the influx of newcomers had to be stopped.

In another book, *The Orphaned Community*, Fortuyn went out of his way to emphasise his tolerance — of everything other than Islam's intrusion into Dutch society and its 'Jewish-Christian-humanistic culture'. He lamented the anti-Semitism that existed in Dutch society, and insisted that the settling of Jews, Mediterranean, American and other western immigrants brought fewer problems than Muslims, because their cultural heritage was closer to the Dutch one. Even non-Islamic far eastern cultures were easier to assimilate in the US and Europe. He ridiculed the idea of integrating Muslims in areas of Holland which already had high concentrations of them. 'All major Dutch cities know their deprived areas, with an over-concentration of people who came to live in the Netherlands in the last 25 years. By now there are neighbourhoods with more than 60 per cent foreigners by origin, and sometimes you have up to 60 nationalities crowded together. It doesn't need to be explained that integration in such a neighbourhood is an idle idea. Integration into what, when almost everybody comes from abroad and from so many different countries? The original inhabitants who could afford it, moved out, and those who stayed behind are a minority, yet they are more than often treated by politicians as part of a majority imposing its norms and values on minorities!'[3]

His move into politics came in 2001, when he became leader of the *Leefbaar Nederland* (Liveable Netherlands) party. His views on Islam proved too extreme for it, however. He was expelled in February 2002 after giving an interview to the *Volkskrant* newspaper in which he suggested the anti-discrimination article in the Dutch constitution should be abolished, and blamed Muslims for the problems of Dutch cities, including a rising crime wave. 'Moroccan boys never steal from Moroccans. Have you noticed that?' he said, and added: 'It's not very smart to make the problems bigger by letting in millions more immigrants from rural Muslim cultures that don't assimilate. This country is bursting. I think 16 million people are quite enough.'

The furore caused by his interview, and his expulsion from *Leefbaar Nederland*, was the kind of publicity he thrived on, however. He immediately formed a new party — though it was effectively no more than a collection of supporters who formed his 'list' for local elections in Rotterdam in March. The LPF triumphed, taking 35 per cent of the votes and capturing 17 of the council's 45 seats. This was in a city where almost half of the population is of non-Dutch extraction — largely immigrants from north Africa and Turkey.

In the two short months between his victory in Rotterdam and his murder just before the general election in May, Pim the outsider became a major irritant and worry for the political establishment. He was a beaming, genial presence on television. He would end his speeches with a cheery salute and his catch-phrase, in English: 'At your service!' When he had a urine-filled pie slapped in his face by protesters in a television studio, viewers felt genuinely sorry for him, and his stature rose. After his death, mainstream politicians such as the outgoing prime minister, Wim Kok, did not just condemn the killing; they sounded as if they understood that in terms of charisma and presence they were pygmies alongside Pim Fortuyn.

*

Fortuyn's rise to political stardom was truly spectacular. Suffice to say that a study of European far-right parties published in 2000 does not even mention him.[4] His success can in part be explained by the fact that his brand of extremism was not at all like that of traditional far-right parties, in the mould of Le Pen or Haider. Such parties also existed in the Netherlands, the main one being the misnamed *Centrumdemocraten* or Centre Democrats, but even their electoral high point, 2.5 per cent of the votes in 1994, was only half the average level achieved by extreme right parties in other west European countries in the eighties and nineties.[5] The party, led and completely dominated by Hans Janmaat, has only around 2,000 members, of whom at most 100 are activists.

The relative weakness of the Dutch far right has baffled commentators. On the face of it, Holland has the same pre-requisites as other countries: there is a large immigrant population, surveys show a considerable degree of xenophobia, there is cynicism at the 'eternal coalitions' produced by the political system and thus ample scope for a protest vote. Janmaat himself is a well-known figure.

What he lacked, however, was the political skill to run a well-organised party, with a coherent strategy. His election programme in 1994 was a wacky mix of xenophobic and populist proposals ('policies' would be too grand a word for them). They included 'stopping discrimination against the Dutch' and ending immigration, putting asylum seekers in labour camps, introduction of the death penalty, promotion of Dutch products, and lowering the cost of living — including setting the price of petrol at an arbitrary 1.50 guilders a litre.

The Centre Democrats' pamphlets and statements were generally regarded by the Dutch press as ravings, scarcely worth reporting. Pim Fortuyn, by contrast, had the advantage of being a well-known media figure before he decided to enter politics. Almost certainly unintentionally, he did echo some of their views — the notion, for example, that the 'blame' for creating a multi-cultural society in Holland lay not so much with the foreigners themselves as with the 'clique' of established parties who allowed immigration to happen and then tried to cover up the problem by placing a taboo on discussing the issue. With his broad-appeal defence of Dutch liberal values, and his intellectualisation of the 'threat' posed to them by Islam, Fortuyn introduced an element of sophistication to the anti-foreigner arguments. It enabled many Dutch people to espouse xenophobic arguments without making them *feel* right-wing or extreme; indeed, it appealed to their *progressive* instincts. He also added other populist issues to his portfolio: he spoke to people's concerns about street crime and insecurity, about the failings of the police, about long waiting-lists in hospitals.

In contrast to the Centre Democrats, therefore, Fortuyn offered a more credible option for protest voters. His impact dwarfed anything achieved hitherto by Holland's far right.

✳

The man charged with Fortuyn's murder was an animal-lover. Police investigations showed that Volkert van der Graaf had carefully planned the assassination, by studying information about Fortuyn on the internet, acquiring a 9mm parabellum pistol and ammunition, and driving to the radio studio at Hilversum, where he waited for his victim to finish an interview, then shot him at close range in the car park. Van der Graaf was seen running from the scene and arrested at a nearby filling station. His motive for the alleged killing was bizarre, indeed incomprehensible — connected, perhaps, with Fortuyn's approval of fur-farming (though he had no party policy on the matter). Van der Graaf, a vegan animal-rights campaigner, had a strong objection to factory farming. A few years earlier he had said in an interview that as a boy he had objected to fishing with worms because it was cruel to both worm and fish.

Whatever its intended effect, the murder left Holland spinning in confusion. Its political anchors snapped. The country was united by its horror at the first political assassination of the modern era. But the grief and torment so completely swamped the nausea hitherto induced by Fortuyn's policies — at least in three-quarters of the population — that notions of right and wrong were in danger of being confused. Ethical and political landmarks were lost in the fog, as yet more respectability was conferred on Fortuyn and the party he left behind. He was buried with all the honours of a national statesman. Dutch television's coverage of the funeral service at Rotterdam Cathedral was deferential and extensive, preceded by clips from his life overlaid with the John Lennon song 'A working-class hero is something to be'. He had a glorious send-off, sanctified by the church and dignified by the presence of the country's top leaders, including the prime minister, Wim Kok. The Bishop spoke of how many of the thousands who had turned out were protesting 'against the growing aggression and mindless violence in our society'. But it wasn't just that. Many of the thousands applauded as Fortuyn's hearse passed by them along Rotterdam's main street, Coolsingel. Flowers were thrown, until they covered the vehicle, reminding the television presenter of the scenes at Princess Diana's funeral. After the service, as the white coffin was borne out of the cathedral, there was a surreal mix of sounds: ethereal church music, the pealing of bells, and hundreds of spectators making V-signs and chanting like a football crowd — 'Pim Fortuyn, Pim Fortuyn' — and occasionally breaking into a rendition of 'You'll never walk alone'. It was a chilling scene, a reminder of the reality behind Fortuyn's xenophobic, populist party. The dead leader's two spaniels trotted out of the church, skipping round, looking as lost as the rest of Holland's bourgeoisie.

A third of Fortuyn's supporters were said to be immigrants, despite the fact that his principal policy was to halt immigration. The long queue of mourners snaking around his house in Rotterdam in the days after his death contained many Asian and African faces. One exotic looking lady of Indonesian origin, wearing horn-rimmed sunglasses and holding a glorious bouquet of flowers, said she remembered the assassination of John F Kennedy — and this was the same. A wonderful man was dead: she'd been crying all night.

Fortuyn's 'liberal' reasons for objecting to Islam struck a chord with other mourners. A young white woman filing past his house illustrated her support for him by pointing to her well-exposed cleavage. 'I want to be free to walk about like this,' she said. 'But they come up to me (she meant Muslim immigrants) and swear at me or even spit at me. They've got to learn to live like we do.'

Others used a phrase I had first encountered in Vienna when Jörg Haider shot to prominence: Fortuyn had 'broken taboos', he had dared to address subjects that had been swept under the carpet for years, he had shattered the 'politically correct' view of the world that had asserted itself as the only admissible view in Holland, while in the real world trouble, and unanswered questions, were piling up.

That view was held even in strongly immigrant areas. In a cafe near the Feyenoord stadium in Rotterdam, Turkish men who had spent most of their lives in Holland said things about more recent immigrants which would have made Fortuyn blush. 'There's too many of them, too many. They're murderers, they rob banks, they commit all sorts of crimes,' said one, in a heavy Dutch/Turkish accent. 'It's not safe for us to go out in the streets.' These men were not particularly devout Muslims: they attended the mosque only occasionally. They were the kind of assimilated immigrants whom Fortuyn was happy to accept in Holland — and they in turn supported his view that 'enough was enough'.

Fortuyn also accepted immigrants in his party — indeed, several of them, often dismissed as 'token blacks', rose to prominence. When tens of thousands of mourners filed silently through the streets of Rotterdam the evening after Fortuyn's murder, the procession was led by Joao Varela, a 27-year-old businessman born in the Cape Verde islands, who was number two on the party's election list. The woman who lasted but a day as a Fortuyn List minister,

Philomena Bijlhout, was of Surinamese origin. Fortuyn, however, had always stressed he had nothing against foreigners if they adapted totally to the Dutch way of life — and both Cape Verde and Surinam are Christian countries.

Varela was the very opposite of the kind of immigrant against whom Fortuyn railed. He had come to Holland at the age of six with his father, a guest-worker at Rotterdam's Van Nelle coffee factory. Aged eight, Joao ran away from home and was fostered by a Dutch family. He was an outstanding athlete — a Dutch tennis champion — and used his winnings to pay his way through Rotterdam's Erasmus University, where he studied economics. Tall and dapper, he became a marketing analyst for a cosmetics company, and took the initiative to join Fortuyn's new party in February 2002 by calling him at home and offering his services. The chance of a smart black assimilated Dutchman, a devout Catholic, to offset charges of racism, was too good to be missed: Fortuyn snapped him up and made him his deputy. Varela said he joined the party out of personal admiration for Fortuyn and the challenge he mounted to mainstream Dutch politics. As a self-made man, he took the rough edge off the party's xenophobic profile: Varela said he wanted to inspire other immigrants to make good of their lives in the Netherlands. 'The Netherlands does have a problem with asylum seekers, refugees, illegal and other immigrants,' he said. 'I'm fully behind Fortuyn on this. Stop people coming in for the moment till we can sort out this conflict.'[6]

Varela pointed to the vast arrays of satellite dishes in immigrant areas, and shops with Arabic signs, trading in imported goods, as evidence of Holland's poor integration policy. Too many Turks and Moroccans were still looking to home for their comforts, instead of doing what he had done — adopting a new homeland and adapting to its traditions.

*

About 10 per cent of Holland's 16 million population are described as 'non-western' immigrants, and the decade from 1992-2001 brought in a further 360,000 — legally, plus many more illegally. Pim Fortuyn undoubtedly benefited from growing discomfort among the indigenous population, which intensified in the wake of the September 11th attacks. An opinion poll found that large numbers of the population were in favour of the deportation of Muslims who supported the attacks whilst others were keen to see asylum seekers with Muslim backgrounds being refused entry to the country. The poll itself was criticised as an example of sensationalist news management (it appeared, in the *Volkskrant* newspaper, under the headline, 'Radical Muslims to be Expelled'), which may have added to the negative atmosphere.[7] Existing extreme right groups were quick to exploit the mood: the small Populist Party used explicitly Islamophobic language, while the New National Party took the opportunity to launch a new recruitment drive. But it was Fortuyn, with his articulate turn of phrase and his flamboyant touch, who prospered most in the new climate.

Islam, and its compatibility with western civilisation, came under scrutiny as never before, and that 'achievement' of Fortuyn continued after his death. In July 2002, the new parliament called for an unprecedented investigation into the beliefs and activities of the country's 800,000 Muslims, following a television report on the behaviour of four imams. Nova, a respected and far-from-right-wing current affairs programme, secretly recorded the clerics making statements which prosecutors believed might have broken the law by inciting violence. In one case, an imam in the Hague called on Allah to 'take care of' President George W. Bush and the Israeli leader, Ariel Sharon', while another in Amsterdam praised Palestinian suicide bombers. A third made derogatory remarks about women. It led MPs to instigate a study of the funding and management of the country's mosques and the training of clerics, with a view to discovering how many Muslims could legitimately be classed as fundamentalists. The new government was considering how to school imams in

Dutch values, including homosexuality and women's rights, and whether to license only those born in the Netherlands.[8]

It does not take a Pim Fortuyn to persuade Dutch people that the imams' views are totally at odds with 'the Dutch experience'. Even the spokesman for a Muslim lobby group in the Netherlands admitted that the general public would 'mostly remember these bearded men talking about hitting women and praying to God to punish Sharon'. So, if the fear of fundamentalism — and to some extent of Islam itself — is shared by a majority of Holland's liberal and libertarian people, does it mean that Fortuyn was right to 'break taboos' and come out against it? Did he reflect the mood correctly? (The election result suggests he did.) And was he therefore wrongly maligned in other countries and by Holland's own left-wing politicians? The answers to these questions are not easy. To answer 'yes' is to imply that Fortuyn's 'liberal fascism' is a sustainable — or even progressive — system of Western values, perhaps even a model for other countries. It has certainly heavily influenced the political debate in Holland itself, as witnessed by the new immigration law, and not dissimilar policies are being pursued in other parts of the European Union, even by mainstream politicians who at the same time would go out of their way to declare Fortuyn's policies anathema, and denounce the discriminatory or racist rationale behind them.

175

Yet xenophobia, when it comes down to it, is xenophobia, however attractively packaged in a 'liberal' philosophy. The key to this conundrum lies in whether one believes, like Fortuyn, that progressive Western values really are under threat from Islam. For him, defending them was the same as protecting democracy from Nazism in the thirties: appeasement would mean allowing democracy (or in this case, Holland's permissive society) to go under. But *is* there such a threat from Islam? Particularly since no Islamic power is threatening to invade Europe! Are 800,000 peaceful Muslims — many of them perfectly well integrated — actually a threat at all to the Dutch way of life? Or was Professor Pim ultimately a racist, exaggerating the risk because, perhaps, as a homosexual he was particularly sensitive to any threat to his freedom? His intellectual arguments, laid out in several books and endless television appearances, persuaded more than a million Dutch voters, making him one of the most influential (as well as the most complex) of populist politicians in Europe. One can only guess at what progress he would have made if he had not been killed.

Pim Fortuyn had a love of things Italian. His villa in Rotterdam was named Palazzo di Pietro. He had a holiday home in the village of Provesano di San Giorgio in north-eastern Italy, and it was there that he was reburied, in a white marble sarcophagus, after being transferred from his temporary resting place at the Westerveld cemetery in

Driehuis on 20 July 2002 — a day or so before his supporters were sworn into office in the new Dutch government. The grave became an instant shrine for far-right enthusiasts, many of whom may have underestimated the complexity of this very Dutch variety of fascist. One suspects the enthusiasm may wane, as Pim Fortuyn's 'party' crumbles, and his ideas become more and more 'ordinary', with mainstream parties taking them on board and making them 'respectable'.

For that, ultimately, may prove to have been Pim Fortuyn's main contribution: to have legitimised racism and xenophobia by exaggerating the danger posed to Dutch society by Islam. He personally may have had the intellectual ability to distinguish between racism *per se* and his very particular, closely focused arguments. But his followers, and others influenced by his policies (not to mention the government, now implementing them), may be less sophisticated, turning Holland away from its decades-long traditions of tolerance and enlightenment for the sake of fighting a non-existent threat.

Notes

1 Election statistics available in *NRC Handelsblad*, 24 May 2002.

2 *The Guardian*, 7 May 2002.

3 Pim Fortuyn, *De verweesde samenleving*, Karakter Uitgevers B.V., 2002, p. 187.

4 Paul Hainsworth (ed.), *The Politics of the Extreme Right*, London: Pinter, 2000.

5 *Ibid.*, p. 159.

6 *The Guardian*, 10 May 2002.

7 *NRC Handelsblad*, 27 September 2002.

8 Andrew Osborn in *The Guardian*, 9 July 2002.

7.

Belgium — Europe's Hole in the Head

On Sunday 25 August 2002 thousands of Flemings[1] gathered in the small town of Diksmuide for the 75th annual 'Yser pilgrimage', a commemoration of the bloody Battle of the Yser in the First World War, when thousands of Flemish soldiers lost their lives — partly, it is said, because they could not understand the instructions of their French-speaking Belgian commanders. Their graves, and now a large monument in this little town in West Flanders, were marked with the letters AVV-VVK: Everything for Flanders, Flanders for Christ. The annual pilgrimage has always been a highpoint in the Flemish nationalist calendar, with the soldiers revered as early martyrs for the cause of independence from Belgium. An inscription on a grassy hill where one of the battles was fought reads: 'Here lie their bodies like seeds in the sand, hope for the harvest, oh, Flanderland.'

For many years the event was dominated by the ultra-nationalist Vlaams Blok, and was usually attended, on the sidelines, by a variety of far-right, fascist and neo-Nazi groups from around Europe. But recently the organising committee decided to shed the pilgrimage's extremist image. This year they had made clear the Vlaams Blok was not welcome. The programme of poetry, song and dance was dedicated to 'Peace, Freedom, Tolerance', which was claimed to be the soldiers' true testament. The event was still a celebration of Flemish nationhood, and speakers demanded autonomy for Flanders. But tolerance was the watchword, and at one point a group of Kurds — also a nation in search of nationhood — was even invited to perform a song. *Foreigners* performing at a Flemish nationalist outing! It was unheard of — and some of the elderly people in the audience looked less than enthralled by this intrusion into their annual display of patriotism.

The authorities had taken the precaution of banning counter-demonstrations. But just outside the main arena, held back by ranks of riot police, the Vlaams Blok was nonetheless there. Waving Flemish flags — bright yellow, with a black lion rampant — they jeered and whistled at the Kurds, mocked their style of singing, and tried to drown out the proceedings with chants of 'Sack Lionel' (Lionel Vandenberghe being the chairman of the Yser Pilgrimage committee). Lurking at a safe distance, pretending not to be a part of this ugly demonstration, but doing nothing to hinder it, was Filip Dewinter, the party's secretary general, and main leader. He is one of Europe's 'designer fascists', with views and a deep suntan to match those of Jörg Haider. When I asked him about the attempt to disrupt the gathering, he dismissed it as a 'small incident, nothing important' and explained his objections to the new-style Yser pilgrimage: 'Ten or twenty years ago we used to have thirty or forty thousand people here, but then people from the government parties infiltrated the organising committee and tried to moderate the speeches. Now we have a Flemish demonstration without real political statements. That political statement, the testament of those frontline soldiers, should be: independence for Flanders, nothing more, nothing less. But they don't want that. They're talking about everything now — they even had a Moroccan pop group playing here once, and they're talking about a multicultural society and tolerance and peace and whatever — but not about what really happens about Flemish independence.'

I had never heard anyone use the words 'moderate' and 'tolerance' as negative concepts before, but Dewinter said the words mockingly. 'Multicultural' he said with a sneer.

We said goodbye and he continued to mill around in the sunshine with his supporters, browsing through stalls selling nationalist literature and Nazi memorabilia. There were war veterans wearing hearing aids and young children with Vlaams Blok pennants. At one stand, you could buy books about Hitler or the Waffen-SS, or the *Gestapo and SS Manual*. Just down the road a dozen skinheads burned Belgian flags or publicly urinated on them. Above, a police helicopter droned, and some in the crowd raised their beer glasses ironically to this symbol of Belgian state oppression.

*

Belgium, created in 1830, was a flimsy kind of unified state from the outset. It has always been an anomaly: a Belgian diplomat described it to me as the little hole in the European skull, where the bones didn't quite fuse properly together when nations were being formed. Years of oppression of the Flemings by the French-speaking elite did nothing to encourage their loyalty. At one time the country's administrative, managerial and professional ranks were filled almost entirely by French-speakers, even in Flanders. To this day there are certain Flemish families who speak French at home.

There was a time when the French-speaking southern half of the country, Wallonia, with its thriving coal and steel industries, was more prosperous than the rural, Flemish, north. Now coal and steel production is in steep decline, while the Dutch-speaking Flemings have the high-tech and service industries that make it the more prosperous part, encouraging a feeling among many that they are being dragged down by their Walloon fellow-countrymen. The division of Belgium grew deeper in the sixties, when an official linguistic boundary was established. After student protests in 1968 the ancient French-speaking university in the Flemish city of Leuven was split into two, with a Dutch-language one remaining in the city and a French one exiled to a new town in Wallonia known as Louvain-la-Neuve. All Belgian political parties split into separate Flemish and francophone parties. Starting in 1970, a series of constitutional changes divided the country into three regions (Flanders, Wallonia and bilingual Brussels) and increasingly federalised Belgium. But for Flemish nationalists the changes were insufficient. The Vlaams Blok was founded in 1977 to defend Flemish interests and fight not just for devolution but for separation — the creation of an independent Flanders.

The Blok has become one of Europe's most hardline and xenophobic far-right movements. It forms a faction in the European Parliament with Germany's Republikaner and France's National Front. Its leaders consort with Austria's Jörg Haider and lapse into anti-Semitism. Its policies include the repatriation of all non-European foreigners. Electorally,

Year	Election	Votes	% in Flanders
1978	National	76,000	1.8
1981	National	66,000	1.5
1984	European	73,000	1.3
1985	National	85,000	1.9
1987	National	116,000	3.0
1989	European	241,000	6.6
1991	National	405,000	10.4
1994	European	464,000	12.6
1995	National	476,000	12.3
1999	European	598,000	14.8
1999	National	613,000	15.4

it has gone from success to success, its share of the vote increasing steadily year after year, as the table above shows.

In local and provincial elections it has done even better. In October 2000, the party received 32.8 per cent in its heartland, the city of Antwerp, 26.3 per cent in nearby Mechelen and 21.9 per cent in Ghent. Since voting is compulsory in Belgium, it means that between a quarter and a third of the adult population in these cities made a conscious choice for an overtly anti-democratic party. If it were not for the *cordon sanitaire* — the solemn pledge of all other parties to eschew any kind of cooperation or alliance with the Vlaams Blok, its leading light, Filip Dewinter, would be mayor of Antwerp, and the party — which jumped ahead of the Socialist Party to become the third-biggest in Flanders in 1999's national elections — might well be on its way to governing the province, and breaking up Belgium.

At a May Day rally of the party faithful in Bruges in 2002 the Vlaams Blok chairman, Frank Vanhecke, mocked the portrayal of the party in the media: 'Dear friends and fellow dung beetles, savages, peripheral morons, vultures, rats, rotten apples, narrow-minded elements turned sour, extremists, politically incorrect anti-democrats, brown-shirted scum and members of militias... welcome to my city!' Vanhecke, one of the Blok's two members of the European Parliament, lashed out at the party's critics: 'They call the Vlaams Blok a danger for democracy, whereas our long series of victories is an expression of our people's demand for democracy. We are called intolerant, but it is the "*cordon sanitaire*" that is intolerant. They say we preach hatred, but they are the ones who hate us.' But Vanhecke made no bones about his kindred spirits in Europe's other far-right movements which had recently triumphed in elections: 'After Austria, Spain (*sic*), Italy, Scandinavia, the Netherlands and France, the apparatchiks and commissars of the left, who have nested in politics and the media and who thought of themselves as the centre of the universe, shiver. It is a pity there are no elections in our country this month. The French and Dutch are going to the polls. Although every country is different and you cannot just equate Jean-Marie Le Pen or Pim Fortuyn with us, we have become in each of our countries the only hope for native citizens who have been under-appreciated, patronised and held in contempt.'

Vanhecke's attempt to sound moderate belied the reality of a strongly xenophobic party. Its ultimate aim appears to be a racially pure, separate Flanders. As a means to that end it proposes the transfer of all federal powers (though there are few of them left) to the regions, and — pending the repatriation of non-European foreigners — the creation of a separate social security system for immigrants and the abolition of their right to vote in local and European elections. It claims that government employment policies discriminate in favour of immigrants and against Flemings. It says it respects foreigners who 'make an effort to adjust as *guests*' — but condemns, for example, the provision of interpreters to help immigrants in homes for the elderly, as 'special treatment'. It fought the 1999 elections under the slogan: 'Baas in eigen land' (In charge of our own country).

The Institute for Jewish Policy Research, in its reports on anti-Semitism around the world, has pointed to racist remarks made by Vlaams Blok members of the European Parliament. In 2001 the party's vice president, Roeland

Raes (the former distributor of a neo-Nazi magazine, *De Schakel*), caused a scandal by casting doubt on the scale of the Holocaust. He was asked in a Dutch television interview whether he doubted that the gas chambers had really existed on a grand scale. Raes replied: 'Yes, I dare to doubt that. I think that what we've been given to believe on certain points has been very exaggerated. The persecution and the deportation of the Jews did take place in a systematic way. But whether it was planned that everyone was going to die — well, that's another question.' He was also sceptical when asked whether he accepted that six million Jews had been murdered by the Nazis. 'Of course it does seem that a lot of serious things did take place — with the Jews, with the gypsies and also with homosexuals. But to come up with an exact figure, well that's a completely different question.'[2] The remarks — which also suggested that the diaries of Anne Frank, the Jewish schoolgirl who hid from the Nazis in wartime Amsterdam, might have been fakes — were seized upon by the press as proof of the Vlaams Blok's real nature. 'A mask falls and the Vlaams Blok grimaces,' said a headline in *La Libre Belgique*. Raes was forced to resign from his post, and the party leadership hastened to distance itself from his comments, which could make him liable to prosecution under a 1995 law against Holocaust-denial.

Belgium has the highest number of immigrants per head in the European Union. Many of them originated in the country's former central African colonies, while others came from north Africa and eastern Europe. In the decade of large-scale immigration associated with the wars in Yugoslavia and the Middle East, from 1992-2001, Belgium received a yearly average of 22,000 asylum seekers, which a country of only ten million struggled to absorb. Antwerp, the party's stronghold, has a substantial Jewish population, connected with its bustling diamond trade, and neighbourhoods dominated by Moroccans. The Vlaams Blok has consistently used the foreign presence to stir up racial intolerance.

A study of the Blok's election manifestoes over the years shows, however, that less and less prominence has in fact been given to the issue of immigration — presumably because, as the party's prime and well-known policy, there was less need to stress it — while more was given to crime and to corruption in government and public life.[3] A series of scandals had dogged the country since the late eighties. The Agusta affair — the discovery of an alleged 50m BF ($2m) bribe to secure a major government contract for the purchase of army helicopters — brought down ministers, while leading members of the francophone Socialist Party (whose leader, André Cools, was murdered in 1991) also became embroiled in corruption, and several were found guilty of fraud and embezzlement. In the 1994 European elections the Vlaams Blok's slogan was 'Big House Cleaning'. Public anger with the authorities — all grist to the Blok's mill — was compounded in 1996 as a notorious paedophile scandal developed. Marc Dutroux had been released from jail in 1992 after serving just three of a 13-year sentence for the abduction and rape of under-age girls. Now he was re-arrested after the discovery of four girls' bodies on his property and of two more, alive, whom he admitted to having kidnapped. The investigation — including the failure of police to discover two of the girls before they died when they 'searched' Dutroux's house — was marked by bungling, incompetence and allegations of corruption. To make matters worse, Dutroux escaped from police custody briefly in 1998: heads rolled in the government, and the Vlaams Blok cashed in on the public's growing disillusion with the political establishment.

The city of Antwerp had specific factors which turned it into the most fertile ground for the far right. In the immediate post-War years, many Flemings who had been accused or suspected of collaboration with the Nazis gravitated towards the country's largest Flemish city seeking anonymity. They provided financial and other support for the Vlaams Blok in its early years.[4] The city suffered more than most from Belgium's elaborate system of party patronage, similar to the *Proporz* system in Austria, under which the Christian Democrats and the Social Democrats had parcelled out jobs and funds unchallenged since the twenties. Belgium's leading expert on the far right, Marc Swyngedouw, observed that 'city officials are promoted not on the basis of their skills, but because they are regarded as belonging to the right party at the right time. Subsidised housing, jobs, and preferential treatment in numerous organisations and services must be obtained via the party organisation, itself controlled by a small elite. In some areas, dynasties have emerged, with central functions in the apparatus passed down from father to son.'[5] By the late seventies, when the Vlaams Blok was created, this Catholic-socialist monopoly was thoroughly discredited, as Antwerp suffered from administrative incompetence, corruption, and growing social problems. The influx of largely Moroccan and Turkish guest workers in the sixties and seventies meant local people in deprived areas found themselves competing with foreigners for housing and jobs. The incomers were often poorer, had more children and were more often unemployed than Flemings, and therefore often qualified for subsidised housing — giving Belgian applicants the false impression that the foreigners were receiving favourable treatment.

In 1988 Filip Dewinter, a hardliner and a skilled demagogue, took over the organisation of the Vlaams Blok in Antwerp. He set up cells of activists in deprived neighbourhoods, who organised protest actions against immigrants, targetted Muslim prayer houses and mosques, and promoted the idea that foreigners were primarily to blame for crime and unemployment. At the same time Dewinter loosened the Blok's association with former Nazi collaborators and strove to present it as a modern, respectable party. Over the following decade its popularity in the city soared.

Like many of Europe's populist parties, the Vlaams Blok has exploited the changes that have taken place over recent decades in society: the emergence of multicultural communities, the dislocation caused by post-industrial economic change and the degeneration of mainstream coalitions that have ruled unchallenged for too long. As Swyngedouw concludes: 'The likely losers in this structural transformation are young, unskilled, blue-collar workers, lower-middle-class employees and small businessmen. These are the categories which have sought salvation in the Vlaams Blok, which has offered them the simple but misleading illusion that once all the immigrants have gone, the prospects for welfare and the certainties of the past will all come flooding back.'[6]

*

Xenophobia has soured the atmosphere in the more nationalistic Flemish districts of Belgium where substantial numbers of foreigners live — not just in places like Antwerp, but even in some areas near Brussels where the foreigners are largely other Europeans, associated with the

European institutions. I happen to live in the suburb of Overijse, just outside Brussels proper, in Flanders. Registering to live there, as one is obliged to do, was a daunting experience, as all staff at the 'commune', or local council office, have been instructed to speak only Dutch — even to foreigners who have just arrived. When I approached the officials, with a smile and a 'Does anyone here speak English, please?' I was greeted with hostile stares from everyone in the room and a brisk shaking of heads. I had little option but to carry on in English, which, it emerged, the officials understood perfectly, but to which they replied only with nods and grimaces, and eventually a stab of the finger towards a notice which informed visitors that 'to preserve its cultural and linguistic identity Overijse is a Dutch-language-only commune', and that Dutch lessons were available at such-and-such an address. We struggled on, and my family was duly registered, but it was a frosty, unwelcoming event. It is the only place I have ever come across where people who speak English — the world's lingua franca — refuse to do so even to communicate with foreigners. Incidentally, this is purely state-sponsored xenophobia: it exists only within the local authority offices, whereas Flemish neighbours and shop-assistants in Overijse are happy to use English or French if a foreigner is struggling with Dutch. I can make no direct link to the Vlaams Blok — except that the commune does make itself available for its demonstrations — but this, it seemed to me, was a taste of what a Flanders run by the Blok would be like.

Even worse are the leaflets and Vlaams Blok newspapers pushed through my letter-box. The February 2002 edition of *De 'Eigen Volk Eerst'-Krant* (Our Own Folk First-Newspaper) had the headline: 'Foreigners' right to vote — never!' For the first time it struck me that I, as much as any black African or Muslim, was a target for the Vlaams Blok's message of hate. The paper argued over several pages why foreigners should not be allowed to take part in Belgian elections. The most telling reason seemed to be that, in the Blok's view, most foreigners would vote for French-speaking candidates (and it was for this reason, it said, that the idea was allegedly supported only by Francophone Belgians).

The newspaper featured an interview with a former Miss Belgium, Anke Van dermeersch, to lend glamour to the xenophobia. She began by explaining that she had nothing against foreigners, indeed, she was married to one... from Luxembourg. But she complained Belgium was now the easiest country in the world to settle in, thanks to the so-called *snel-belg-wet* ('fast-track citizenship law') — a one-off amnesty for illegal immigrants granted for a three-week period during October 2001, when aliens who had been in the country for at least six years were offered legal residence documents. The law, Ms Van dermeersch said, 'had allowed criminals from the east

European mafia and Islamic terrorists to acquire Belgian identity cards.'

Getting into her stride, she went on: 'It bothers me a lot that a number of things just can't be talked about any more in this country. Everyone knows that there are enormous problems with foreigners who get into crime. Everyone sees that the younger generation of foreigners sets itself against any form of authority (the police, etc) and against our Western values. More and more often, our girls and women, when they're out in the street or in the trams, are insulted, or touched, or even assaulted. So I think the future is bleak. And the fact that more and more Muslim girls wear a headscarf is not hopeful for integration. As a woman I am concerned. ... The Vlaams Blok has been saying for a year and a day that foreigners — not just north Africans but east Europeans too — are responsible for a large part of the crimes committed. ... Hospitality is one thing, but we mustn't be crazy. There's been so much moaning recently about tolerance. I think we should say once and for all that that has to come from both sides. Because I don't want to go back to the middle ages. I don't want to have to go out in the street with a veil on tomorrow.' It sounded almost like incitement to white people to go out and rip the *hijab* (headscarf) from the heads of Muslim women.

The alleged imminent Islamicisation of Belgium is standard dogma in the Vlaams Blok. At a barbeque for party members in the small town of Torhout in August 2002, Dewinter was introduced by the chairman with the words: 'Here is Filip Dewinter, who will address you in one of Belgium's four national languages.' (This was a reference to a call by a radical Muslim leader in Antwerp — himself perhaps as extreme as Dewinter — for Arabic to be made an official language along with Dutch, French and German.) 'I predicted that this is how things would go!' Dewinter roared. 'It's because we never showed them our fist and put a stop to it.' He noted the 'segregation of swimming pools for men and women' for the sake of Muslims (in fact, this happens for only one hour per week, and was requested by a Catholic women's organisation as well as an Islamic group, for women who prefer to bathe alone), the alleged 'banning' of pork in state schools (simply not true, according to the city authorities), and a request for Arabic television to be subsidised by the government. 'Give them a finger and they will take an arm, and a whole body.' Dewinter was now pummelling the air with his fists, descending into sheer fantasy as his rabid rhetoric took over. 'That is why it is our historic task to stop the conquest by the hordes on Europe's borders, who want to put the crescent moon on our churches and city halls.'

Dewinter's style is almost a definition of populism. 'We just say what people think,' he told me. 'A lot of political issues and themes are taboo at the moment — it's impossible to speak about the immigrant problems, it's impossible to speak about the rise of crime. The politically correct parties don't want to speak about these things. We just say what people are thinking about this sort of issues, and that's the reason our party is doing very well. We are a non-conformist, non-traditional political party.' What is missing in such an approach is the sense of responsibility that a mainstream party exhibits — an awareness that a political party actually has to do more than simply parrot the uninformed ravings of the football stand. On the contrary, the Vlaams Blok thrives on public ignorance and prejudice. If telling the people that Flanders' Catholic churches are about to be turned into mosques wins votes, then it is worth saying.

*

What holds Belgium together? In many ways the two communities lead separate lives, with their own television and radio stations, separate educational systems, and mutual suspicions. They do share a religion, Roman Catholicism, and it is sometimes said that the royal family is a uniting factor — but for most people that is just a symbol, with little impact on their daily lives. It is true that few Flemish people would wish to be united with the (Protestant) Netherlands, and neither would the Walloons wish to become a *département* of France — but that is not a very positive reason for the existence of a country of such mismatched halves. Mixed marriages would make a divorce painful. And the capital, Brussels, is a shared asset that would give the lawyers a major headache — it is geographically within Flanders, but assigned bilingual status and in fact largely French-speaking.

Not surprisingly, perhaps, since both are developed Western European nations, a survey in *Le Vif* magazine discovered that Walloons and Flemings shared the same essential values, though with subtle differences.[7] The average income of a Flemish household was €34,480 (about £21,000), in Wallonia just €30,326 (about £19,000). Perhaps because of that, in Flanders more people put free time ahead of work, whereas in Wallonia — struggling to catch up — people tended to value work ahead of free time. Francophones tended to stick to 'old-fashioned' family values — marriage and children — whereas in Flanders people are having fewer children and marrying less. Fully twice as many Flemish women believed they could be happy without children compared to French-speaking Belgian women.

On the crucial question of xenophobia, a different study found, in 1998, that a higher proportion of Belgians generally regarded themselves as racist, than any other European nation. But *Le Vif*'s survey suggested more hostile attitudes in the north of the country — Vlaams Blok territory. Some 25 per cent of Flemings did not wish to have a Muslim or foreign worker as a neighbour, whereas only 15 per cent of Walloons held such views. A little more than 55 per cent of Flemings were unconcerned by the conditions of life of foreigners, only 43 per cent in Wallonia. This helps to explain the relative lack of success of the Blok's 'equivalent' in the south, the *Front National*, a francophone anti-immigration party which has only one seat in the federal parliament, compared to the Blok's fifteen.

The chasm between the two nations is certainly growing, and the Vlaams Blok is prising it wider and wider open. Though not in power anywhere, it has a disruptive influence disproportionate to its size. This is because the *cordon sanitaire* — the necessity of keeping it out of government — obliges all or most other parties to come together to form often unwieldy coalitions. This is the case both in Antwerp and in the Flanders regional parliament. There is an argument that the policy of keeping the Vlaams Blok in quarantine tends to make it more and more extreme, or at least provides it with no incentive to become more moderate, since it knows it will never be allowed into government and actually have to implement its policies. It exists in a hypothetical realm and can just appeal to people's base fears and prejudices in the hope of finally winning such an electoral success that it can break through the *cordon sanitaire* and govern on its own. Looking at its spectacular growth over the past fifteen years, it would be foolish to discount the possibility of that happening.

Dewinter takes heart from Jörg Haider's achievement in finally breaking the policy of *Ausgrenzung* — being shunned by the mainstream parties — in Austria, but is realistic about how long it will take in Belgium. 'Within the next five to ten years it will be possible, I think. Probably not at the next [federal] election [in 2003], but in 2006 with the next local elections I think we will have the opportunity to break the *cordon sanitaire*.'

Notes

1 The Flemish people, or Flemings, comprise about 60 per cent of Belgium's population and live in the northern part of the country (Flanders). They refer to their language as Dutch: 'Flemish' does not exist as a separate language, but is merely a dialect of Dutch. The southern part of Belgium is known as Wallonia and is inhabited by Walloons, or French-speaking Belgians. About 1 per cent of the population, in the east of the country, speak German.

2 *The Guardian*, 9 March 2001.

3 Stefaan Walgrave, Knut de Swert, 'Does news matter? The contribution of the news media in the making of the issues of the Vlaams Blok', a paper presented at a conference in Torino, March 2002.

4   Marc Swyngedouw, 'Belgium: The *Vlaams Blok* and Antwerp', in P. Hainsworth, *op. cit.*, p. 134.

5   *Ibid.*, p. 122.

6   *Ibid.*, p. 141.

7   *Le Vif*, No. 19, 2002.

8.

Denmark in a Right State

In the summer of 2002 I had one of my strangest
encounters with a politician. It was Constitution Day, the
5th of June, and Bertel Haarder, immigration minister in
Denmark's centre-right coalition government, had come to
a tiny village near Vejle in eastern Jutland to address an
open-air gathering organised by the local branch of the
centre-right Liberal Party, of which he was a member. It
was a relaxed, sunny afternoon, but Haarder, a tall, rather
gangly man, turned up late from a previous engagement
and seemed rather on edge about his interview with the
BBC. I had come to ask him about Denmark's new
immigration law, which had recently been passed by
parliament (with the help of votes from the far-right

Danish People's Party) and was due to come into force on
1 July. It had come in for much criticism, from journalists,
human rights activists and even the government of neighbouring Sweden, for turning what was once one of
Europe's most welcoming places for asylum seekers into
one of the most difficult for foreigners to get into. Even in
the months preceding its introduction — just in anticipa-
tion of it — asylum applications in Denmark had halved,
while those in Sweden, seen as the next best thing, had
doubled. Its provisions were variously described as
'draconian', 'drastic', 'illiberal' and even 'racist', and I was
keen to hear how the minister would justify them. To say
he was touchy, would be a huge understatement. The
following are the main points of the new law:[1]

> o Welfare benefits for asylum seekers are slashed by up
> to 50 per cent
> o Claimants must wait seven, rather than three, years
> for a permanent residence permit and the right to full
> benefits
> o They have no right to marry during that period
> o Asylum seekers are to be deported immediately if
> their application is rejected, not, as previously, after 15
> days
> o Refugees with no permanent residence permits will be
> returned to their country of origin if the government
> deems it to have become 'safe'

o There is no automatic right to family reunion: the right of parents over 60 to come to Denmark is abolished

o No Dane — immigrant or otherwise — is allowed to bring in a spouse from outside the EU if either husband or wife is under 24; that precludes a young American, for instance, from joining a Danish husband or wife.

We stood in a leafy garden for the interview, while the party faithful waited in the sun for their guest speaker. My first question, about the instant deportation of failed asylum seekers upset Haarder at once. He offered this stumbling definition of the word 'instant': 'It's not instant deportation. If you get your asylum application refused then ... of course ... the person has to go home ... without too much delay.'

I moved on to another issue — the right to marry foreigners under 24. 'Are we talking about deportation or the right to marry?' he snapped back.

'Both,' I replied, 'I just want you to explain why you felt it necessary to adopt this law. It has proved controversial, after all.'

'No, it's not controversial,' he retorted.

'Well,' I said, 'the Swedish government isn't too happy: their social affairs minister, Mona Sahlin, sent you an official complaint.' 'Pah,' snorted Haarder, 'she doesn't know what she's talking about.'

Neither did I, it turned out, for even though I had a heavily perused and underlined copy of the law and accompanying documents printed off from the government's own website, Haarder accused me of being badly prepared. He also did not like the people I quoted to him. When I mentioned Bashy Quraishy, president of the European Network Against Racism (who had described the law as 'racist'), Haarder retorted: 'If you speak to people like that, you'll understand nothing.'

As soon as the interview was over, the minister started stomping around the garden with his arms flailing like a bad impression of Basil Fawlty. 'I have never been asked such questions,' he shouted. 'How could you ask me such things... It's as if I would ask you whether you... sexually abuse your children!' It was impossible to calm him down.

By eleven o'clock that night Haarder had tracked down my mobile telephone number and rang me to continue his rant. His reaction was all the more puzzling because many Danes had told me they regarded him as a 'decent chap', the best in the new right-of-centre government. The only conclusion I could reach was that he was under immense strain trying to defend legislation about which he himself perhaps had his doubts.

The law ended Denmark's tradition as one of the most hospitable countries in Europe. Over the previous ten years it had received almost ten thousand asylum seekers a year — equivalent to 1.84 per thousand inhabitants. That put it sixth in the league table of recipient countries, and well above Britain (eleventh, with just 0.97 asylum seekers per thousand inhabitants). Only Switzerland, Sweden, the Netherlands, Belgium and Germany received more, per head of population, than Denmark. Not that this made it 'overcrowded': immigrants (other than from Europe and the USA) account for only about 5.6 per cent of the country's 5.3 million population.

New arrivals are accommodated in 51 small asylum seeker centres run by the Red Cross, while their claims are dealt with. At the one I visited, at Stensbaek in southern Jutland, 120 refugees cooked their own meals, and did voluntary (unpaid) work, producing furniture, greenhouses, and the like. They were free to come and go, but not to work elsewhere — they received allowances which were very generous by most countries' standards. Their children were bussed to a nearby Red Cross school each day. They lived in small flats, with basic furniture and televisions, from which they struggled to glean the facts about the new asylum laws. Most were from Bosnia or Afghanistan. All said they hoped for a 'better life' in Denmark, and many described the bloody ethnic strife back home from which they hoped to escape. Once their claims were accepted, the refugees would be moved out of the centres into the community where they could find proper jobs.

Denmark was rightly proud of its treatment of asylum seekers. Compared to many other countries, immigrants were remarkably well-integrated, although unemployment among incomers was high. The vast majority of asylum seekers from countries such as Iraq — to which it would be impossible to return them without endangering their lives — were accepted after only the most cursory of interviews. (In November 2001 procedures were tightened, after the Danish police's intelligence service reported that Denmark was being used by Iraqi agents pretending to be refugees.)

But one incident in the year 2000 inflamed passions and contributed to a major change in Denmark's attitude. A young girl was raped by a gang of immigrant teenagers in Copenhagen, fuelling fears that rising crime was largely due to 'foreigners'. Controversially, during the election in the late autumn of 2001, the Liberal Party used a picture of the rapists leaving court with their heads shielded under coats on one of their campaign posters, with the slogan, 'It's time for a change'. Immigration became a major issue, and the Liberals swept to victory on their promises to crack down on it.

To many, though, it seemed that the Liberals were jumping on a bandwagon set in motion much longer ago by the Danish People's Party (*Dansk Folkeparti*), led by Denmark's answer to Le Pen or Haider — the rather schoolmarmish Pia Kjaersgaard. I caught up with her, too, on Constitution Day, at an outdoor People's Party gathering in the town of Assens, on the island of Funen. Her largely middle-aged supporters sat drinking beer and eating hot dogs outside a red-tiled park pavilion. A dais was set up beneath a Danish flag and *DF* posters saying 'Vote Danish'. The party symbol is really nothing like a swastika at all — it is curved, not jagged — but its red, white and black design has uncanny sub-Nazi undertones. So did the singing of national songs as the crowd waited, and then the leader made her way to the podium, escorted by blond young men bearing tasselled red-and-white standards on staves with arrow-head points. She made her speech about the imperative of keeping the Danish Constitution superior to EU laws. Later, as we chatted about the new immigration law, she expressed her delight that her ideas had now been adopted as government policy. 'The trouble with foreigners,' she told me, 'is their religion, their customs, their traditions, and the fact they don't speak Danish. It is hard to integrate them.' Having won 12 per cent of the vote and 22 seats in the 175-member parliament, the People's Party was in the rather comfortable position of not being in the government coalition, and therefore bearing no responsibility, while wielding enormous power as the party on which the Liberals depended for a voting majority. No wonder Bertel Haarder was squirming: his government was effectively implementing hardline anti-immigrant policies devised by the populist right.

✷

It was not the first time Pia Kjaersgaard had achieved a major change in Danish policy without being in government. Two years earlier, when Denmark held a referendum on whether to join the European single currency, she had led the anti-euro campaign. The entire political establishment — the then ruling Social Democrats, the main opposition parties, the trade unions, employers, and the bulk of the media — was in favour of joining. But on polling day, 28 September 2000, 53 per cent voted against. That was largely due to the campaign run by the People's Party on the far right and the June Movement on the left.

The Danish People's Party emerged as a splinter group of the anti-tax Progress Party, which back in 1973 had achieved almost 16 per cent of the vote, but had steadily lost influence ever since. Its founder, Mogens Glistrup, had a colourful, populist touch. In his first television appearance, in 1971, he praised tax evaders as being like railway saboteurs during the German occupation. He proposed to abolish Denmark's defence forces in favour of a telephone answering machine with the message, in Russian: 'We surrender'! He suggested selling off Greenland and the Faeroe Islands to the highest bidder. (None of these ideas was actually adopted as Progress Party policy.)

Pia Kjaersgaard was one of the Progress Party's few MPs when she led a defection of about a third of its members in

1995 to create the People's Party. She hoped to establish a softer approach, aimed at the possibility of entering government as a respectable coalition partner. The two organisations remain similar in outlook, although the People's Party's greater emphasis on immigration and the EU appears to have been successful in making it predominant on the far right, while the Progress Party's focus on economic liberalism earned it only 0.6 per cent in the 2001 elections, and no seats in parliament.

The People's Party can probably be said to be less extreme than the others described so far in this book. Kjaersgaard avoids the demagoguery of Le Pen, the pro-Nazi lapses of Haider, the crude racism of Bossi. She leads what has been described as a 'radical right-wing populist' party,[2] which appeals to ordinary people and their fears, warning for example that Denmark's cradle-to-grave welfare system cannot withstand mass immigration. Foreigners and the European Union are its twin obsessions.

The top article in the Danish People's Party's programme is entitled 'Foreigners and Native Rights', and it sets out a typically 'Danes first' agenda. 'Denmark is not and has never been,' it contends, 'a country intended for immigration, and the Danish People's Party disagrees with the statement that Denmark will develop into a multi-ethnic society.'[3] Asylum may be given to refugees 'to a limited extent' and subject to annual review. 'Attempts

211

should not be made to integrate these refugees into Danish society, but on the contrary they should be sent home again once the conditions in their own countries make this justifiable.' The police should be able to refuse unfounded asylum seekers at the border; criminal foreigners must be expelled permanently; tough measures must be taken to stop pro-forma marriages; the right to bring in family members should be ended; and tuition in an asylum seeker's mother tongue should be abolished. Much of that was achieved when the new Danish government — of which the People's Party was not a member — brought in its immigration legislation in 2002. Indeed, in some respects the law went further. Its restriction of the right of any Dane to marry a non-EU foreigner if either of them was younger than 24 was regarded by many as truly bizarre. Pavel Seidenfaden, the editor of the daily *Politiken*, told me: 'What's happened here is we have tried to moderate xenophobia by becoming half-xenophobic ourselves. I think we will pay a high price because xenophobia is not like a tax policy where you can move up five points and get it right; it is something that has to do with our relationships among human beings, and therefore notching that rhetoric up actually hurts the whole underlying problem of how to live together in a society that's more diverse than in the past.'

The second article refers to the European Union, to which the party 'is deeply opposed'. Here it strikes a

212

resonant chord in Danish society, one of the most euro-sceptic in the EU. Voters chose to join the European Union in a referendum in 1972, but thereafter repeatedly rejected moves towards closer integration. (They accepted the Maastricht Treaty on European Union only on a re-run of the vote, after Copenhagen had secured opt-outs from contentious clauses.) Kjaersgaard would like the EU reduced to a mere free trade area, with no joint decision-making in foreign affairs, defence or monetary and financial policies. Her party calls for the European Parliament to be disbanded and the Commission reduced to a mere civil service. EU regional funds and the wasteful agricultural policy should be 'wound up'.

Kjaersgaard herself is scarcely a firebrand orator. A small, serious blonde lady, she makes her speeches in an even tone. Perhaps it is her apparent level-headedness that appeals to voters. But what she lacks in rabble-rousing ability, she makes up in tireless touring of the country during every political campaign. She seems oblivious to her tendency to teeter on the verge of racism. In 2000, a campaign group which helps unemployed immigrants launched a poster pointing up the racism in Danish society: it showed a black youngster and the caption, 'When I become white, I'll be a schoolteacher'. The Danish People's Party responded with a controversial parody, claiming that foreigners can jump the queue for state housing. Their poster showed a homeless white man and the caption: 'When I become a Muslim, I'll have a home'. The advertisement provoked an outcry. 'Hitler and Pia Kjaersgaard are of a piece,' exclaimed Peter Duetoft, an MP for a small centre-right party: 'I am not saying she is a Nazi, but she has the same attitude of dividing the population into superior and inferior people as Hitler did.'[4]

Kjaersgaard revealed her colours again in August of the following year when her party took out a full-page advertisement in the *Jyllands-Posten* newspaper to publish a 'name and shame' list of five thousand immigrants who had recently been given Danish citizenship. Her opponents described the list as 'vindictive', but she brushed aside the criticism, saying she merely wished to show her people who the 'new Danes' were, adding, 'And they are not Europeans or Americans. They are people from outside that area.'

September 11th brought an upsurge in anti-Muslim activity, in which the Danish People's Party was directly involved — to the extent that some its members were reported to the police for violation of Section 266b of the Criminal Code (for 'hate speech'). One, Mogens Camre, a member of the European Parliament, was quoted by a newspaper as telling the party's Annual General Meeting: 'All countries of the Western world are infiltrated by Muslims — some of them speak to us politely, whilst they wait until they are enough to kill us all.' Another member,

Michael Rex, said: 'Islam is not a religion in a proper sense. It is a terrorist movement.' A third, Kenneth Kristensen, was reported as saying: 'In Denmark you are not allowed to say things how they are — to call a spade a spade — call a so-called second-generation immigrant that which he is, a dense (*sic*) deviant. The fact is that the majority of these young Arabs are criminals who, with their worshipping of violence and their intense hate, continue the traditions their parents have given them.'[5]

Thus, a direct link was made between terrorism and Islam, and a blanket inference drawn that immigrants in Denmark were in some way connected with the attacks on New York. Pia Kjaersgaard herself stated that Islam should be fought intensely because of its fundamentalist tendencies. Abetted by such statements and by a press described by EU racism monitors as 'already drenched in negative stereotypes of Islam and Muslims', there was a dramatic upsurge in verbal and physical threats against identifiable Muslims, such as women wearing the *hijab*, as well as incidents of graffiti, arson and firebombs against Muslim property. An opinion poll discovered that the vast majority of the population felt that Muslims should be made to take lessons in Danish democratic values.[6]

The terrorist attacks, and the ensuing anti-Islamic feeling, had a direct effect on the general election campaign which ran through November. Although mainstream parties distanced themselves from the hate-inspired talk of the far right, 'foreigners' became the central issue, with the question of immigration, kept under wraps by mainstream governments for years, finally pulled out into the open. This led, as we have seen, to the Social Democrats being voted out of power and replaced by a right-wing coalition supported by the People's Party — and the adoption of Europe's tightest immigration laws. Admittedly, most of the EU was moving in the same direction. The new Liberal prime minister, Anders Fogh Rasmussen, pulled a wry face when I suggested to him that the new legislation had caused great controversy: the wind, he believed, was blowing in the Danish direction. And he was right.

*

The debate brought to the fore the question of what it meant to be Danish, and indeed European, in this age of mass migration. As *The Economist* pointed out, 'Denmark has been a strikingly homogeneous society. Well out into the centre-left, few politicians see merit in multicultur-alism. What they want is assimilation: let the immigrants be any colour, but let them think and act like decent Danes.'[7] It is a question that most European societies are having to face: to what extent do we wish to benefit from the variety and positive values that immigrants can bring, and to what extent do we expect them to 'become' European, that is, in effect, to give up — or weaken their allegiance to — their own religions, cultures, languages and values? Does 'integration' mean more than merely respecting your new country's laws? Does it mean giving up traditions and values which may be a fundamental part of you, but upset some of your new neighbours? Or is multiculturalism — tolerance of differences, and the diversification of a country's make-up — the way forward?

The Danish People's Party knows the answer. It is simply to keep Denmark reserved for white, preferably Christian, Danes. But for many incomers who have settled in the country and love it and respect its values, the change in policy has come as a rude awakening. Roya Moghaddas Hoffmeyer, an Iranian married to a Dane, who has lived in Denmark for 25 years and heads the Federation of Ethnic Minorities Organisations, told me she was devastated to find that 'they make us feel inferior, a burden on society. I would never have believed it: Denmark was such a liberal country.'

I put that message to the immigration minister, Bertel Haarder, during our interview about the new law: 'In Denmark you used to be considered so liberal...'

'Still are!' he roared at me, 'Still are! Just compare us with your own country. You'll find out. Very liberal, very tolerant, no racism, no groups that throw bombs or anything. This is an inclusive society, and this legislation will make it even more inclusive.' And with that he stomped off to address his meeting.

Notes

1 See 'A new policy for foreigners' on the Danish government website.

2 Jørgen Goul Andersen and Tor Bjørklund, 'Radical Right-Wing Populism in Scandinavia', in Paul Hainsworth, *op. cit.*, p. 200.

3 This and other quotations from Pia Kjaersgaard, 'The Fundamental Programme of the Danish People's Party: Introduction', www.dansk-folkeparti.dk.

4 *The Economist*, 3 February 2000.

5 European Monitoring Centre on Racism and Xenophobia, 'Anti-Islamic Reactions in the EU after the terrorist acts against the USA: Denmark'.

6 European Monitoring Centre on Racism and Xenophobia, 'Summary Report on Islamophobia in the EU after 11 September 2001'.

7 *The Economist*, 22 November 2001.

9.

Britain's Bulldog Kept on a Leash

Studies of the far right in Britain tend to focus less on the danger it poses than on explaining why its influence is so low — weaker than almost anywhere else in Europe. Support for the two main movements, the National Front and the British National Party, has indeed never been strong enough to cause great concern about the threat to democracy. But the available statistics demonstrate a clear correlation between the far right's success at any given time and the political hue of the government of the day (see chart).[1]

Britain's largest post-War far-right party, the National Front, reached its peak membership (14,000 members) in

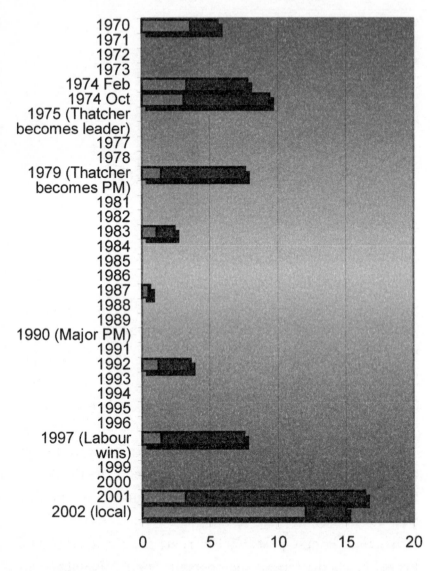

GENERAL ELECTION PERFORMANCES BY
NF (UP TO 1983) AND BNP (FROM 1987)

■ Avge % vote, in seats contested   ■ Best result

1972 and had its best performance in a general election in October 1974, when it won 9.4 per cent in one constituency. The following year, Margaret Thatcher became leader of the Conservative Party, and in 1979 she won her first election, ushering in eighteen years of right-wing rule that stretched the concept of 'mainstream right' to its limit. During the Thatcher period the National Front's membership and its electoral success dwindled, until it polled just 0.6 per cent in 1987 and fell apart. The far-right cause was meanwhile taken up by the British National Party (founded in 1982 by the NF's former leader, John Tyndall), but it too scraped along at the bottom of the polls.

When Mrs Thatcher handed over to the less strident John Major in 1990, the BNP's performance began to improve, rising just slightly in the early nineties, until 1997 — the year the Conservatives lost by a landslide to Tony Blair's New Labour — when it scored an average of 1.4 per cent, but 7.5 per cent in its best constituency. In 2001 the BNP scored 3.2 per cent in the constituencies it contested, and its new leader, Nick Griffin, took 16.4 per cent in the northern constituency of Oldham West. A year later the party put in its best performance in local elections, with three councillors elected in Burnley, Lancashire, and an average of 12 per cent in the 66 seats they contested.

The correlation, though doubtless simplistic, makes sense. The far right has done best under Labour governments, and has struggled to exist during those years when many of its policies — or approximations of them — were in any case being championed by the Conservative government of the day — strongly by Thatcher (with her talk in 1978 of foreigners 'swamping' British culture, which brought Conservative gains in opinion polls) and somewhat less so by Major. The rise in support during the nineties may also reflect the widening appeal of far-right policies on immigration, just as was seen in Germany and other countries during the same period, when the numbers of asylum seekers and illegal immigrants were growing.

*

The National Front was eclipsed by the British National Party in the eighties, but it still exists, and both organisations produce copious amounts of literature and merchandise, and also run websites, through which they hope to gain publicity largely denied them by the mainstream press. The differences between the two are fairly superficial, as a commentator in *The Guardian* observed: 'The NF was more unashamedly neo-Nazi, with its shaven heads and bovver boots. Its strategy, like the Hitler followers of the *bierkeller* era, was pubs and streets first, votes later. The BNP is a little cleverer. It tries to present a respectable, scrubbed face. It talks, as does the French National Front, about crime and fear and "the kids' future". Of course, we know what they're really about. We know this is just a new form of the virus, evolved to survive better.'[2]

The virus, essentially, is racism. It pervades the policies of both groups, but especially the National Front, which openly describes itself as a 'white nationalist movement'. The Front's website includes a section entitled 'The NF Fallen List: Some of the many hundreds of British victims of coloured immigration and government-enforced multi-culturalism.' It lists 150. For each violent death described, the only motive given is a reference to the skin colour or ethnicity of the alleged perpetrator. The victims are invariably described as having been quietly going about their business, while the attackers are 'Negroes' or 'half-breeds' and intellectually inferior. A few extracts:

> Alan was gunned down at close range after answering his front door. He struggled with a Negro attacker and was helped by his wife Lauren to get the man out of his home. A second Negro appeared, pulled out a gun and shot Alan. The Black killers fled on foot. Alan was taken to Newham hospital but died soon after his arrival...
> ... Mrs Cutress is another of countless elderly victims to be mugged & murdered by savage low IQ street Negroes, let into our country by

treacherous Labour & Tory politicians in the last fifty years.

Tony, a window cleaner and father of one child, was walking along Orpington High St with his girlfriend in the late evening on the Saturday over the Golden Jubilee bank holiday when he was jumped on and beaten to death by three savage Muslim thugs in an unprovoked violent racist assault. He died the next day in Queen Mary's Hospital, Sidcup, from serious head injuries. Insanely the three Asian murderers, kebab shop workers Hasan Kebene, Adnan Hussein and Hasson Burunlu have all been released on bail against the Crown Prosecution Service's advice. How long before these foreign racist killers disappear abroad as has happened in so many similar murder cases? This extremely vicious racist murder received minimal local news coverage and no national coverage, which is becoming more and more common when the victim is White!

Father of two John was quietly drinking in the Piano & Pincher pub, when loud-mouthed half-breed Winston Richards launched a unprovoked violent attack.

... At the trial it was discovered that one of the Negroes had been adopted at birth by a white liberal middle-class couple, which once again opened the debate over Nurture vs. Nature, proving yet again that you can take the Negro out of the jungle but you can't take the jungle out of the Negro.

... Unbelievably the judge found him guilty of murder but because the wog suffered from a schizoid personality he gave him only an 8-year prison sentence.

Apart from the overriding aim of ending Britain's multiracial society and repatriating foreigners, the Front's policies purport to aim at nothing more sinister than to devolve powers to local councils, to let parents control schools, and 'to give working people a say in the running of larger companies, rather than being treated merely as cogs in a machine run by absent owners' — almost a socialist paradise! On Europe, predictably, the Front says: 'We do not want a European Super-State. We do not want the Euro. We want to be governed by ourselves. And not by the Germans and French!'

The point is, the National Front's policies are of little interest to anyone. The party exists not as a serious political force nowadays but as a disruptive element, intent on whipping up racial tension in the interests of furthering its 'white nationalist' goals. The British National Party is slightly more sophisticated. In the last local elections in

2002 it put up 68 candidates — targeting only those seats where it had a measure of support — and campaigned on a recognisable slate of policies. Its programme proposes an isolationist 'Britain first' solution to the country's problems, and is unashamedly extremist and populist in every detail. Immigration is the number one issue:

> On current demographic trends, we, the native British people, will be an ethnic minority in our own country within sixty years. To ensure that this does not happen, and that the British people retain their homeland and identity, we call for an immediate halt to all further immigration, the immediate deportation of criminal and illegal immigrants, and the introduction of a system of voluntary resettlement whereby those immigrants who are legally here will be afforded the opportunity to return to their lands of ethnic origin assisted by a generous financial incentives both for individuals and for the countries in question. We will abolish the 'positive discrimina-tion' schemes that have made white Britons second-class citizens. We will also clamp down on the flood of 'asylum seekers', all of whom are either bogus or can find refuge much nearer their home countries.

On Europe, the BNP, too, advocates withdrawal from the EU. Its crackdown on crime would end the 'liberal fixation' with the rights of criminals, and bring back flogging for petty criminals and vandals and the death penalty for paedophiles, terrorists and murderers. The prospectus hankers after a golden age before supermarkets and globalised world trade, and aims to exclude foreign-made goods, encourage small-scale farming and restore the UK's exclusive fishing zones. Foreign aid ('subsidising the incompetence and corruption of third world states') would be ended and the funds redirected to Britain's health and social services. The party thus tries to appeal not only to young people, particularly those living in deprived areas with large immigrant communities who can be made scapegoats for unemployment and crime, but also to older people with rose-tinted memories of a more glorious British past.

*

Both parties are rooted in a fairly weak British fascist tradition that goes back to Oswald Mosley's British Union of Fascists, which grew to a maximum membership of fifty thousand in 1934 but made little impact on elections at either local or national level. After a war fought against German Nazis and Italian fascists, there was no appetite at all for extreme right politics, until a whole generation had passed. It was not until 1967 that the National Front was founded, as a 'patriotic' movement aimed not just against multiracialism and mass immigration but against 'capitalism, communism and internationalism', all three of which it claimed 'took power away from the individual'.[3] Their extremist policies were lent a degree of legitimacy by Enoch Powell, the prominent Conservative MP, who also called for the 'voluntary' repatriation of non-whites and in a speech in 1968 predicted 'rivers of blood' if immigration was not curbed. The NF saw a small but steady rise in influence throughout the seventies, mainly at local or by-elections. In a 1972 parliamentary by-election in the West Bromwich parliamentary constituency, for example, an NF candidate won 16 per cent, while in local elections in Leicester in 1977 Front candidates polled almost 20 per cent of the vote. Later that year NF demonstrators clashed in London with thousands of anti-Nazi protesters, but the Front revelled in the publicity. The established parties clearly recognised the threat. In December Labour devoted a party political broadcast to an attack on the National Front, and the Anti-Nazi League was set up — backed by a number of celebrities — to draw attention to the Front's unacceptable racism. The following year Margaret Thatcher made her speech about 'understanding' the fears of British people being swamped by coloured immigrants. The Front saw that as an attempt to siphon off support. The concerted adverse publicity certainly had an effect when it came to the 1979 general election: the National Front's performance was abysmal, and it never recovered.

In 1980 its leader John Tyndall was squeezed out of the National Front and two years later he founded the British National Party. He hoped to make the new party more 'respectable' than the old one, partly by throwing off its bovver-boy image and appealing to disillusioned Conservatives. But with Thatcher in her prime there were few of them about, and the BNP failed to make much impression throughout the eighties. Inner-city race riots in 1981, 1985 and 1991 may have helped the party to highlight its cause. In 1993 it scored its first electoral success, when Derek Beacon won a council seat on the Isle of Dogs with 34 per cent of the vote, after campaigning on a 'Rights for Whites' platform. The reasons for such a high endorsement of a fairly mediocre and inarticulate candidate have baffled academics,[4] but it seems to have been partly a protest vote, perhaps a reaction to John Major's new grey brand of Toryism, perhaps connected with the first influx of refugees from Bosnia, and partly the result of local conditions in a borough where racial tension had been bubbling after the apparently racially motivated killing of a white youth. At any rate, the BNP man did not last long. He was voted out a year later.

Tyndall proved to be an ineffective leader. He failed to conceal his past enthusiasm for Nazism, and his magazine, *Spearhead*, advertised Holocaust denial material. So it was

231

not until a new brand of leader came along — in the shape of the smooth, articulate, Cambridge-educated Nick Griffin — that the BNP finally achieved a breakthrough. For the 1999 European Parliament elections he helped the party shape a more moderate image, dropping the idea of compulsory repatriation, for instance. The renamed party magazine, titled *Freedom*, sounded kitten-like on the race question: 'The BNP does not claim that any one race is superior to any other, simply that they are different. The party merely wishes to preserve these differences which make up the rich tapestry of humankind.' That might, admittedly, involve building walls between the ethnic communities in places like Oldham or Burnley. The new parlance did not persuade observers such as Professor Roger Griffin (no relation) of Oxford Brookes University: 'Nick Griffin is trying to modernise the BNP by adopting the language of right-wing leaders such as Le Pen in France and Haider in Austria. But under the cloak of loving difference, there is essentially a Nazi-style hatred of racial inferiors.'[5]

A little excavation of Nick Griffin's past suggested this was true. A member of the National Front until 1989, he left Cambridge with a law degree and a boxing blue, and travelled to Libya to solicit (unsuccessfully) funds and advice from Colonel Gadaffi on how to set up 'people's committees' — NF grass-roots cells. In the nineties he advocated defending rights for whites 'with well-directed boots and fists'. A Holocaust denier and anti-Semite, he published a booklet entitled 'Who Are the Mind Benders?' which outlined a Jewish conspiracy to brainwash the British people in their 'homeland'. In 1997 he was caught on camera (in a set-up, which led him to believe he was speaking to representatives of the French National Front) complaining: 'Britain does not have the tradition of intellectual fascism which is such an important factor in many other countries. While I do have a number of proposals to help rectify this deficiency, the truth is that this is a handicap which we can never overcome completely.' He added that the BNP should not try to appeal to 'middle-class notions of respectability... It is more important to control the streets of a city than its council chambers.' In 1998 he received a two-year suspended sentence for distributing material likely to incite racial hatred.

By the time of the 2000 general election, however, a year after becoming leader of the BNP, Griffin had transformed himself outwardly into a 'moderniser', a respectable besuited politician who lived on a smallholding in Wales with his wife and four children, raising pigs and chickens — and campaigning on populist issues: getting tough on paedophiles, saving Sterling, and exploiting any other issue that came along.

One such opportunity arose in May 2001, just a few weeks before the general election, when five hundred Asian youths fought police over a weekend in Oldham —

where Griffin was standing as a candidate. The BNP had already caused trouble in the town by starting a 'boycott Asian businesses' campaign, and white thugs had been seen on Saturday nights trying to provoke Asians. Both police and politicians were quick to blame the rioting on the far right for stirring up race hate. Richard Knowles, the Liberal Democrat leader of Oldham council, said: 'Their tactic is to heighten the tension, provoke a reaction and then withdraw. So all the media messages are then of Asians battling with the police. Then the BNP and NF say, "We told you so".'[6] And sure enough, Griffin's response to the rioting was to call it 'inevitable' and to propose segregating the communities as the only answer. His message clearly struck a chord among Oldham's intimidated residents. He won 16.4 per cent of the vote in the Oldham West constituency, pushing the Liberal Democrats into fourth place. At the declaration of the result, he stood with a gag around his mouth to protest at the cancellation of the traditional post-election speeches, lest he use his to stir up yet more trouble.

The attacks of September 11th, carried out by 'Islamic fundamentalists', provided the BNP with an even better opportunity to incite ethnic strife. It launched what EU monitors described as a 'highly explicit Islamophobic campaign'. This stressed the supposed inability of co-existing with Islam and described Christianity as being under threat from Muslims in the UK. The BNP also tried

234

to co-opt Sikhs and Hindus into their anti-Islamic campaign, apparently in the hope of causing trouble between those sections of the immigrant community. The BNP's 'Campaign Against Islam' included a recruitment leaflet which blamed current troubles on politicians who 'forced a multicultural society upon us' and urged readers to join the party for 'the chance to help reverse the undemocratic folly of the old parties and stop the fanatics who want to turn Britain into an Islamic Republic'. A second leaflet, on schools, encouraged parents to withdraw their children from religious studies at school 'to protect our children from multicultural brainwashing', while a third provided a useful mnemonic for ISLAM — Intolerance, Slaughter, Looting, Arson and Molestation of women. BNP leaflets in London claimed churches would soon be turned into mosques if immediate action were not taken.[7]

Out in the streets, a sharp increase in racist violence followed the attacks on New York, which seemed to indicate that the terms 'terrorist', 'Muslim' and 'immigrant' were becoming indistinguishable in some people's minds — just as the far right parties wanted. Muslim women wearing the hijab and men wearing turbans were particularly vulnerable to attack, while Islamic centres and mosques received hate mail, or were daubed with paint or even firebombed. The European Monitoring Centre on Racism and Xenophobia registered scores of incidents. A 14-year-old Muslim boy had his face pushed into a toilet bowl by a gang, who then wrote 'Osama' on his forehead and pushed a sausage into his mouth to break his Ramadan fast. A 20-year-old woman was assaulted on a bus, and called 'Muslim bastard'. In Birmingham a woman had newspaper pictures of the World Trade Centre brandished in her face, and a skinhead wearing a bomber jacket sprayed beer in her face at a busy bus-stop. A young Muslim man with a beard was forced to walk out of his job in a bakery in Wood Lane, London, after continual religious and racial abuse from his colleagues — words like: 'How's your brother, Osama Bin Laden? We're gonna get you Islamic bastards... You're a bloody terrorist, I bet you've got a bomb on your body.'[8]

Parts of the British media contributed to the atmosphere of hatred. The right-wing press had for years been drumming home the notion that immigration was a 'problem', indeed a 'growing problem'. (In fact, Britain ranked eleventh among developed countries in terms of asylum seekers received per head of population, and since 2000 the numbers were decreasing.) The idea that some immigrants might actually contribute beneficially to British society was rarely entertained. Newspapers returned daily to the awful situation at the Sangatte Red Cross centre, near Calais, where asylum seekers waited their chance to jump on to a train or stow away in a lorry bound for England. A picture was built up of 'hordes' of 'bogus asylum seekers' waiting to invade the UK, determined to scrounge off good British hospitality. Now, after September 11th, immigrants were portrayed as 'the enemy within', thanks to the fact that some of the suicide bombers were believed to have resided in EU countries as asylum seekers. There were recurring headlines such as, 'I was born British, but I am a Muslim first'[9], and 'First it's my religion, then my family ... and finally it's my country'.[10] The EU's racism monitors singled out what they called the 'disproportionate' coverage of extremist Muslim groups and British Muslims who declared their willingness to join an Islamic war against the West. Since many of these people had entered Britain as asylum seekers, 'the distance between issues relating to asylum seekers and those of September 11th began to be gradually narrowed, until the two had almost become identifiable as one.'[11]

The British government was criticised by the EU's racism monitoring centre for 'demonising refugees and asylum seekers' after the attacks of September 11th and thereby legitimising racism and xenophobia. Its tough anti-terrorism legislation also proved controversial. In December the government rushed through the Anti-Terrorism, Crime and Security Act, which allowed the authorities to intern without trial non-British citizens suspected of involvement in international terrorism or viewed as a threat to national security. Nine foreign-born men were held for many months under the Act, but in July 2002 the government's own Special Immigration Appeals

Commission branded it as 'discriminatory' as it applied only to foreigners.

In general, the government's immigration policy was inconsistent, as it wavered between Labour's natural inclination to provide sanctuary to genuine refugees and decent conditions for those waiting for their asylum applications to be processed, and its fear of adverse publicity from the press. Its initial policy — of dispersing asylum seekers around the country and giving them vouchers to pay for food, clothes and other essentials — was abandoned in October 2001, following the murder of a Turkish asylum seeker on a Glasgow housing estate, and other attacks elsewhere in the country. Instead, the government announced, it would build special accommodation centres for up to 3,000 people, where they would receive full board, legal advice, and a small cash allowance. They would also be obliged to carry 'smart' ID cards, with their fingerprints and photographs. The home secretary, David Blunkett, described it as 'a radical and fundamental reform of our asylum and immigration policy' — but it was criticised both by refugee workers who suspected the centres would resemble glorified prisons, and by ordinary people terrified by the prospect of thousands of foreigners being dumped on their doorsteps.

The fiasco over Sangatte reached a peak in May 2002 when hundreds of asylum seekers a week were cutting their way through the fences around the rail depot and making their way through the Channel Tunnel. The press went crazy: 'Asylum seekers free-for-all', said the headline in the *Evening Standard*; 'Asylum lunacy', shouted the *Daily Star*; 'Six men on bikes guard us against illegals (four at weekends),' reported the *Sun*. Television news showed endless footage of shadowy figures beetling down the tracks under the yellow sodium lights, reinforcing the impression of an invasion of England by stealth. Blunkett announced he would seek urgent talks with the French government aimed at securing the closure of the Sangatte centre (though whether that would really solve the problem, or just move it elsewhere, was unclear). And Britain suddenly stepped up its rhetoric on illegal immigration. The prime minister, Tony Blair, floated plans for warships to patrol the EU's coastline, for joint border controls, and for sanctions to be imposed against third world countries which refused to take back rejected asylum seekers. The proposals met with such hostility — not only from human rights and aid organisations but from EU partners such as Sweden — that they were quickly watered down. Nonetheless, as we shall see in a later chapter, the EU's immigration policies were to be considerably toughened.

*

Following the BNP's good showing in the 2001 general election, the re-elected Labour government and the new home secretary, David Blunkett, showed greater awareness of the far-right challenge. Before the local council elections the following year, Labour and anti-fascist groups circulated leaflets exposing the criminal records of fifty candidates to be fielded by the BNP. Colin Smith, for example, standing in Bexley, London, had a long list of convictions including theft, possession of drugs, criminal damage, handling stolen goods and possession of an offensive weapon.[12] Blunkett made an appeal to mainstream parties to 'fight head-on' the threat from the BNP and what he called its 'vile racism'. He said it was 'a battle we must enter with urgency, here in this country, across Europe and beyond'.[13] But he himself had been accused of playing into the far right's hands by urging immigrants to learn English and criticising arranged marriages — not because the suggestions themselves were wrong but because they tended to stoke the BNP's fire by implying that they had been right all along to highlight such issues.

And then, just before the elections, Blunkett resorted to that word: 'swamping'. He repeated it so often and refused so resolutely to retract it that one might have thought he was intentionally emulating Thatcher, whose use of the word 24 years earlier probably helped to undercut the then rampant National Front. Now Blunkett too took the word straight from the BNP's lexicon, saying that the giant accommodation centres planned for asylum seekers should provide them with schooling and health care to prevent them from 'swamping' local services.

The remark caused an uproar. *The Independent* argued that Blunkett's 'use of the sort of language you might find in a BNP leaflet simply legitimises the sorts of arguments the far right uses.' Such a tactic might bring short-term electoral advantage, but did long-term damage: 'Mrs Thatcher's stance did nothing to make the case for a multicultural society or prevent the simmering racial tensions that spilled over into riots in the 1980s.'[14] As it happens, Blunkett's intervention did not even bring short-term benefit. A week later, the BNP won three seats on Burnley council. The comment had clearly gone down well in BNP territory. One journalist visited the ward where the party had achieved its best result: 'In Burnley's stone-built village of Worsthorne locals such as Elsie Thornbur, wearing a claret Burnley Golf Club jersey, insisted she did not want "illegal immigration" and said "Blunkett is right — they're swamping our schools".'[15] She had voted not for Labour but for the BNP.

The home secretary made his remark — and defended it in parliament — on the very day that Jean-Marie Le Pen visited the European Parliament in Brussels, triumphant after his first-round success in the French presidential election. He was watched there by an Asian British MEP from London, Claude Moraes, who reflected that Le Pen's achievement was to have made his odious, extreme ideas acceptable by dint of repetition, over many years, and by having them adopted in weaker form by politicians such as Chirac. The same 'mainstreaming' of far-right parties and their ideas was happening across Europe, from France to Austria, from Denmark to the Netherlands. 'See what has happened,' he wrote. 'The acceptability of ideas once considered to be fringe and extreme are now at or near the heart of government, national, regional and local. ... While we [in Britain] do not have the electoral system and the political history that would foster a surge in support for a Le Pen-style party, the danger we must avoid is far-right ideas and rhetoric being absorbed or becoming acceptable in our mainstream politics.' That was why Blunkett had been wrong to adopt the BNP's language. After all, Moraes wrote, 'the BNP is not much interested in asylum policy when it attacks third- and fourth-generation English-speaking Asians of Oldham and Burnley. Toughen up on one policy and they will simply up the ante on the next.'[1]

*

So why has the British far right remained so much less successful than its continental counterparts? The British National Party is not a national force. Its vote at the last general election amounted to just 0.2 per cent of the total, concentrated in one or two areas. It is a local, not a national danger. It is also limited to England, though it is

242

trying hard to make inroads in Scotland and Wales. While warning against complacency, one commentator suggested this might be due to Britain being a more multiracial society, more tolerant and diverse than others: 'The British Election Survey showed that in 1997 only 36 per cent of the public saw immigration as bad for Britain. Some 60 per cent deemed it good for Britain, or were non-committal, and this rose to 86 per cent among those aged under 24. ... In Britain the key outlet for populist nationalism may be euro-scepticism rather than anti-immigrant racism.'[17]

But the BNP also lacks what all the successful European far right parties have — a charismatic leader. Nick Griffin's superficial respectability is no substitute. He does not compare with Le Pen, Fortuyn or Haider (all of whom incidentally were independently rich: they may have appealed to the hard-done-by and oppressed, but they were certainly not of that ilk themselves). Their relative wealth and contacts also helped them secure media access and publicity, whereas the BNP has no influential PR machine and — apart from those rare moments of electoral success — has generally been ignored by the media.

A further difference is Britain's majority voting system, which discourages people from 'wasting' a ballot on minor parties that have no chance of winning, whereas a proportional system gives even small parties some hope of gaining a representative. Perhaps the main reason for the far right's lack of success is that both the National Front and the

British National Party are seen as completely beyond the pale — too rough, too abrasively and *obviously* racist (rather than surreptitiously so, like Le Pen). They come across as oiks and bootboys rather than politicians with a seriously thought-out programme. They may be worth a punt as a protest vote in certain areas at local elections, but few people would trust them in parliament.

✻

As an afterthought — it might almost count as light entertainment were it not so sickening — it is worth mentioning that at the very end of the spectrum small groups of even more rabid fascists exist, though many of them are in jail. Groups such as Combat 18 and Blood & Honour dress up their violence in a veneer of hate-filled 'political' claptrap, but they are little more than ideologised hooligans. The Blood & Honour website reveals that Combat 18 was closely associated with the BNP, until Nick Griffin took it over. 'The British National Party had a brigade of fearless storm-troopers guarding its meetings and demonstrations. They called themselves Combat 18 after our leader Adolf Hitler. Now the BNP is led by an honest man of great integrity with more than a life-time (*sic*) of nationalist activities behind him. But he, or at least his associates, are content with playing the game of democracy where the odds of winning are worse than the mafia's crooked number racket. So when C18 had some ideas of their own, they were promptly given the boot. But the letter-number combination wouldn't go away. It reappeared, and now it had its own life, more vital, nasty, and hungry for the blood of traitors, Reds and zoggies[18] than ever.' The writer discusses the many ways of spreading fear and terror: 'Intimidation, threats and beatings have worked well for the Red bastards for years and years.' He predicts a time when they will release the 'full strike force of the White terror machine'. Many 'patriots', he says, get their training through hooliganism or 'queer and paki bashing': 'It is our job to channel this raw force and fury into constructive Aryan militancy.'

It is no comfort, but perhaps necessary, to know that such evil fantasies and such warped minds exist. Luckily, they are tiny in number.

Notes

1 P.Hainsworth (ed.), *The Politics of the Extreme Right*, p.173; *The Times*, 23 April 2002; *The Guardian*, 9 May 2002.

2 Jackie Ashley in *The Guardian*, 1 May 2002.

3 National Front website.

4 See Roger Eatwell, 'The Extreme Right and British Exceptionalism', in P. Hainsworth (ed.), *op. cit.*, p. 184.

5 Quoted by Rob Chaundy, 'Nick Griffin: Right-Wing Chameleon', BBC Online, 29 June 2001.

6 *The Guardian*, 29 May 2001.

7 European Monitoring Centre on Racism and Xenophobia, 'Summary Report on Islamophobia in the EU after 11 September'.

8 European Monitoring Centre on Racism and Xenophobia, 'Anti-

Islamic Reactions in the EU after the Terrorist Acts against the USA: United Kingdom'.

9 *Daily Mail*, 17 September 2001.

10 *Mail on Sunday*, 23 September 2001.

11 European Monitering Centre on Racism 'Islamophobia in the EU after 11 September 2001', and *The Guardian*, 24 May 2002.

12 *The Guardian*, 11 April 2002.

13 David Blunkett, in *The Guardian*, 11 April 2002.

14 *The Independent*, 25 April 2002.

15 *The Independent*, 4 May 2002.

16 *Ibid.*

17 Peter Riddell in *The Times*, 23 April 2002.

18 ZOG = Zionist Occupation Government.

10.

New Nations and Nationalism

In 1990 there were 159 member of the United Nations. By 1993 there were 184. The majority of the new nations came into being following the disintegration of the communist bloc in eastern Europe, the Soviet Union itself, and the former republic of Yugoslavia. The countries of the Warsaw Pact had maintained the formal attributes of independent countries and as they threw off their communist governments in 1989-90 they were for the most part well prepared to rebuild themselves as nation-states, fired by a reinvigorated sense of identity. In one case, the somewhat artificial state of Czechoslovakia split in two, as the Slovaks sought independence and freedom to assert their own nationhood.

After the 'August coup' which briefly deposed the Soviet president, Mikhail Gorbachev, in 1991, the three Baltic republics of Estonia, Latvia and Lithuania took their chance to break away. Then Boris Yeltsin's determination to assert the supremacy of the Russian Federation (for seven decades the dominant republic of the USSR, and to all intents and purposes barely distinguishable from it) over Gorbachev's Soviet Union, led to his deal — first with Ukraine and Kazakhstan, then with the remaining Soviet republics — that abolished the Union and created a whole new set of ex-Soviet nation states. Within the Russian Federation itself, new nationalisms thrived: nominally Muslim republics such as Tatarstan and Bashkortostan strove to gain maximum autonomy within the federation, while the Caucasian republic of Chechnya took matters into its own hands and declared full independence, bringing upon itself the wrath of the Russian army.

At around the same time Yugoslavia began to disintegrate, with Slovenia, Croatia, Bosnia-Herzegovina, and finally Macedonia breaking away from the Serb-dominated 'rump Yugoslavia' — eventually to be renamed Serbia-Montenegro. All of these emerging nations had fiercely nationalistic leaders, but none more so than Slobodan Miloševic of Yugoslavia, whose attempts to hold on to his crumbling empire and, failing that, to build a Greater Serbia including parts of Croatia and Bosnia, led to the continent's bloodiest war of the late twentieth century.

In many of these cases, nation-building was accompanied by ultra-nationalism, with minorities persecuted and the majorities defending their new homelands with chauvinistic insensitivity.

The following sketches do not pretend to be in any way comprehensive. They are intended merely to give a taste of the kind of threat that has been posed — and in some cases, still is posed — by far-right nationalism in a number of the new countries.

The Baltic States

Little moments remain in my memory from the heady days of 1988-9, when the three Baltic republics first dared to reassert their national identities, before the final break-out from Soviet control. I watched the blue, black and white flag of 'free' Estonia being raised high above Tallinn's medieval castle, watched by thousands of patriots, scarcely believing their own audacity, and scores of Soviet secret policemen, scarcely believing their impotence. In Latvia, demonstrators did something unheard of in those days — they protested against Stalin's deportation of tens of thousands of Latvians to Siberia. All three republics set up 'popular fronts' — this, in a one-Party state — which were embryonic parties struggling for, and eventually gaining, independence. In the Lithuanian capital, Vilnius, the bells of the Catholic cathedral pealed and a massive crowd surged through the streets to celebrate the birth of a new political power, Sajudis, which would lead them to freedom. It was intoxicating stuff. But in each case the seeds of a nasty side of nationalism were also present. The first time a shiver went down my spine was at a concert in Tallinn, where the stage was flanked by Aryan young men in uniforms, carrying flagstaffs, and looking for all the world like direct descendants of the Hitler Youth.

When the three nations finally gained their independence in 1991, they all to a greater or lesser degree began to take out their grudges on the Russians who had subjugated them since the Second World War. The three countries had been assigned to the Soviet sphere of influence under a deal between Hitler and Stalin in 1939, allowing the Soviet army to annexe them in 1940. They were occupied by the Germans during the War, but from 1944 became republics of the USSR. During the decades of Soviet rule it had been Kremlin policy to flood them with Russians and Slavs, both to cement Moscow's political rule and to dilute the indigenous populations, making it more difficult for them to secede. By the 1980s ethnic Latvians comprised less than half of the republic's 2.6 million population (and only one-third in the capital, Riga); Estonians accounted for 60 per cent of Estonia's 1.5 million citizens, and Lithuanians 80 per cent of their republic's 3.6 million.

The new nationalistic governments of Estonia and Latvia passed laws designed to make life difficult for the Russian 'newcomers' — even for those who had been there for decades, and had perhaps been born there — if they had failed to learn the local languages. Lithuania, with far fewer Russians, granted citizenship to all residents, but in Latvia and Estonia, a requirement to pass stringent language tests in order to obtain citizenship meant that half a million Russian-speakers in each country were left stateless. It caused an uproar not just in Russia but among international human rights organisations. Russian-speakers in the north-east of Estonia threatened to take up arms if they were forced to leave the country, and later held a referendum on autonomy. President Yeltsin of Russia accused the Estonian government of practising 'ethnic cleansing' and 'apartheid'. Latvia's initial law automatically gave citizenship only to Latvians and their descendants who had been citizens of the pre-war republic, while naturalisation was possible only after *sixteen* years' residence and a language test — which excluded almost a third of the population.

It was not until 1999 that Latvia — under heavy pressure from the European Union, which it hoped to join — amended its citizenship laws to the satisfaction of human rights groups. In November 2001 Estonia (which had earlier sacked three hundred Russian-speaking policemen who failed language tests) finally adopted legislation scrapping the requirement that candidates for public office must be proficient in Estonian. Even so, large numbers of Russian-speakers in the two Baltic republics remain stateless and therefore excluded from many benefits.

The Baltic states' discriminatory policies were supported by wide sections of the native populations, euphoric at their liberation from Soviet rule, but anti-Russian feeling was particularly whipped up by extreme nationalist groupings, sometimes with historic links to the Nazis. (Many Balts had welcomed the German occupation in 1941 as a 'liberation' from Stalin, who had deported tens of thousands of them to labour camps.) All three countries have been criticised for failing to hunt down Nazi war criminals, and there is still a widespread tendency to forgive the Nazis more than the Russians. In the Estonian town of Parnu 'patriots' wanted to unveil a monument to soldiers who had supported Hitler and opposed Stalin's regime: it portrayed a man in an Estonian Waffen-SS uniform, with a machinegun pointing towards Russia, and an inscription in praise of 'all Estonian soldiers who died [on Hitler's side] in the Second World War for the liberation of the fatherland and a free Europe in 1940-45'. Eventually the city council ordered the monument to be removed and its inscription changed. As the prospect of EU membership draws closer, the Balts are reining in their nationalist instincts.

The Rise of the Far Right

Czechs and Slovaks

For two or three years after the 'Velvet Revolution' that ended communist rule in Czechoslovakia, the country stumbled on as an entity. To the outside world, there seemed little reason for its status to change: Czechs and Slovaks had lived peaceably together for a long time, their languages were different but mutually understandable without any effort, there were thousands of Czech-Slovak marriages and friendships, and the two peoples were joined by culture and a long history. Alexander Dubcek, the leader of the anti-Soviet 'Prague spring' of 1968, was a Slovak, but he'd been a hero in the Czech lands too; Vaclav Havel, the writer-turned-president, was a Czech equally admired in the Slovak eastern third of the country.

I still remember my astonishment, on a visit to the Slovak capital, Bratislava, in 1990, on hearing people arguing — indeed, almost coming to blows — over whether the country (still united at that time) should be named Czechoslovakia or Czecho-Slovakia. That tiny hyphen became a burning, crazy symbol of the nationalism (primarily Slovak nationalism) that was to tear the country apart. (Nothing, of course, compared to the even more bizarre situation that followed the divorce, on 1 January 1993, when Slovakia at least had a name, whereas the Czechs had no real appellation for their country: it consisted of two regions, Bohemia and Moravia, otherwise

255

known as 'the Czech lands', but 'Czecho-' was just a truncated country, a prefix, so to this day it remains the unwieldy 'Czech Republic'.)

The break-up came about largely because of Slovak nationalism, stoked by the populist Vladimir Meciar, a former boxer who created the Movement for a Democratic Slovakia and became the independent country's first prime minister. His rule was controversial from the start, not just because of allegations of corruption and interference in the media, but because of his authoritarian style and inflammatory remarks about the country's large Hungarian and Romany minorities. The Hungarians (almost 11 per cent of the population, and a majority in certain areas) were openly discriminated against by the nationalist government, which removed bilingual signs for town names, insisted that female Hungarian names should carry the Slavic suffix '-ová', and rejected demands for the right to use Hungarian in official matters.

Despite concerns abroad and among human rights organisations at home, Meciar was re-elected in September 1994 with 34 per cent of the vote, and formed an alliance with the extreme nationalist Slovak National Party. Also noted for its outbursts against Hungarians, Roma (gypsies) and Jews, the SNP's leader, Ján Slota, has been a guest at a congress of Jean-Marie Le Pen's National Front. Meꝑiar was finally voted out of power in October 1998, paving the way for a more liberal government.

The treatment of Roma, in both Slovakia and the Czech Republic has been a major cause of concern, and was highlighted in the late nineties when hundreds of them sought political asylum in Canada and Britain following television documentaries that suggested life there would be considerably better for them. Certainly, life is appalling for most of the half a million Roma in the Czech and Slovak republics. They claim they are discriminated against in the allocation of jobs, housing and benefits. Thousands of them live in desperate hovels with no amenities, or in huge, squalid housing estates on the outskirts of cities such as Košice, in eastern Slovakia. Unemployment is endemic, thousands turn to crime, and hundreds have been beaten up by skinheads — and some have been killed by them. Though they have lived in the region for hundreds of years, the Roma are the 'foreigners' of the Czech and Slovak republics, and the targets of the far right. As in the Baltic republics, the hope of joining the European Union has helped to temper nationalist or racist policies. But the disgraceful ghettoisation and mistreatment of the Roma remain a scar on these new democracies.

Russia

If any country in the last few decades fulfilled the kind of criteria that led to the rise of Nazism in thirties Germany, it was Russia. After the collapse of communism in 1991 the country was on its knees. It had lost its status as a superpower: militarily, it had lost the arms race against the USA, and geopolitically it had lost not just the USSR's client states in the former Warsaw Pact, but even regions that had been part of the Russian empire for hundreds of years — the republics of the Caucasus region, the Baltic states, and the Muslim republics of central Asia. Some 25 million Russians found themselves stranded in those outposts, and many of them began flooding back to Russia as the new independent governments of the ex-Soviet republics began to discriminate — intentionally or otherwise — against them. Resentment at such national humiliation was compounded by the economic situation: soaring prices and unemployment, triggered by Boris Yeltsin's 'shock therapy' to turn Russia into a capitalist economy, left millions of Russians below the bread-line. Where Germans in the thirties faced military defeat, economic depression and the challenge of communism, Russians in the nineties faced loss of empire and status, impoverishment, and the threat (as seen by millions) of capitalism. It is to the credit of the Yeltsin government that the country did not collapse into the arms of neo-fascists or nationalist demagogues, for there were many of them around. (And even today, restoring Russian pride and self-esteem is regarded as a major objective by President Vladimir Putin.)

Russia itself was a 'new nation' after the disintegration of the USSR. While the other former Soviet peoples took the first steps towards nationhood by throwing off Russian influences, Russia had to reinvent itself too — by looking back to old traditions and creating new ones. One of the first nationalist movements to emerge — and to display real neo-fascist tendencies — was known as *Pamyat* ('Memory'), led by Dmitry Vasilyev. It began as a campaign to protect churches and other historic buildings, but soon espoused nationalistic and anti-Semitic slogans, blaming the destruction of Russia's environment and archi-tecture on a conspiracy of Zionists and freemasons. In the late eighties it set up groups all over the country and held rallies in factories and parks at which black-shirted leaders made inflammatory speeches. Its thugs smashed up art exhibitions and newly created semi-private restaurants, and created an atmosphere which encouraged many Jews to emigrate.

On the political stage *Pamyat* was soon eclipsed by Vladimir Zhirinovsky's ultra-nationalist Liberal Democratic Party, which was the first party to be officially registered after the Communists gave up their monopoly of power. Founded in 1990, it shot to astonishing success in Russia's first post-communist parliamentary elections in December 1993, winning 22.8 per cent of the vote. Its triumph was entirely due to Zhirinovsky himself, whose antics and policies appalled most people in the West but evidently appealed to almost a quarter of Russian voters. Many years later, Zhirinovsky would admit that his father was a Jew, but at this time he not only denied it ('My mother was Russian, my father was a lawyer') but was openly anti-Semitic, accusing Jews of bringing Russia to ruin. Preying on Russians' fears and resentments after the collapse of the Soviet Union, he called for the restoration of the Soviet empire — and more — saying he dreamt of the day when Russian soldiers would wash their boots in the Indian Ocean. Other outrageous statements included threats to seize Alaska from the United States, to launch a nuclear strike against Japan, to reoccupy the Baltic states, and to flood Germany with nuclear waste. He made a point of visiting pariahs such as Saddam Hussein, Slobodan Miloševic or Colonel Gaddafi, and maintained contacts with most of the far-right parties of western Europe. He promised voters free vodka if they supported him, and notoriously threw orange juice in the face of liberal politician Boris Nemtsov during a television debate.

His success dwindled, though — to 11.2 per cent in the 1995 elections and just 6 per cent in 1999 — as voters turned to more believable options. General Aleksandr Lebed, who outscored Zhirinovsky in the 1996 presidential election, and later Vladimir Putin both offered nationalist, populist solutions without the buffoonery and extremism associated with Zhirinovsky. Russia remains, however, fertile ground for the far right, and that is likely to be the case until its standard of living improves and its status as a world power grows — both of which are priorities for President Putin.

Neo-fascist movements are alarmingly active in society and at lower levels of the state. Back in 1999 the Helsinki human rights group described the southern province of Krasnodar as 'the saddest example of a regime of extreme xenophobia and racial discrimination'. The governor of Krasnodar province, Aleksandr Tkachev, declared 'those with names ending in *ian*, *dze*, *shvili* and *ogli* [i.e. Armenians, Georgians, Meskhetian Turks and Azeris] illegal' and called for the deportation of non-Slav minorities. He authorised Cossacks, the ancient defenders of Russia's borders, who have staged a remarkable revival as part of the nationalist movement since the end of the USSR, to act as police 'auxiliaries' against 'foreigners'. His anti-Semitic predecessor, Nikolai Kondratenko, was rewarded by President Putin with a medal 'for services to the motherland' and a place in the upper house of the Russian parliament.

Racist attacks against black people and against natives of the Caucasus (Georgians, Azeris, Chechens, for example) are common in Moscow and other cities. The city authorities in Moscow have themselves frequently demonised 'Caucasians', accusing them of black-marketeering and crime, and attacks against Chechens increased considerably after the war in Chechnya began in 1994.

Surveys have found that two-thirds of Russians believe Caucasians should be banned from entering Moscow and other major cities. There is much sympathy for official police raids on markets, aimed at expelling Caucasians found without the correct papers, and even for the terrible 'pogroms' occasionally staged by gangs of racist thugs against them.

The most threatening neo-Nazi organisation was the *Russkoye Narodnyoe Yedinstvo* (Russian National Unity) led by Aleksandr Barkashov, a former leader of *Pamyat*. Its symbol incorporated a swastika, and its members, who wore camouflage uniforms and black berets, used Nazi-style salutes. Barkashov indoctrinated his adherents in anti-Semitic, militaristic propaganda. In 1999 some two hundred of them marched through Moscow, though they were forbidden to hold a Congress there. The following year he tried to stand for president in 2000 but was disqualified for technical reasons. The movement, which may have had as many as ten thousand members, split, and Barkashov was expelled from his own party.

President Putin, in an address on 18 April 2002, described the rise of extremism as a 'serious menace to public security and the stability of the country. I am referring above all to those who organise pogroms and beat people up for the sake of slogans or fascist and extremist symbols.' Two months later the Russian parliament adopted a law which allows the ministry of justice to suspend organisations suspected of extremism or of 'endangering state security'. Ironically, the authorities in Krasnodar tried to use it against a non-governmental organisation for trying to alert the media to a hunger strike by Meskhetian Turks ('extremists'). It remains to be seen whether the law will also be used against the real racists — including the authorities in Krasnodar.

Belarus

The president of Belarus, Aleksandr Lukashenka, has been described as Europe's last dictator. His qualifications for the title include fixing elections and changing the constitution to guarantee the prolongation of his own rule, squashing dissent and controlling the media, state control of the economy, and an abysmal human rights record — including allegations of organising death squads to eliminate political opponents. He was first elected president of the country in 1994, three years after it gained independence from the USSR. Two years later he held a referendum that extended his five-year term by two years, and in 2001 was elected to a further five, in elections described as undemocratic by outside observers. He exhibits signs of megalomania, aspiring to reunite Belarus with Russia, apparently in the hope of becoming president of the unified state. Among his friends he claimed the former Yugoslav leader, Slobodan Miloševic, and vowed there would be 'no Kostunica in Belarus' (a reference to Miloševic's democratically elected successor). He runs the economy along scarcely reformed Soviet lines, which has led to chronic shortages of basic goods and foodstuffs. The 1996 referendum allowed him to get rid of an awkward parliament and replace it with a hand-picked one. His security forces have ruthlessly crushed dissent, while sacked government ministers have been harassed or jailed. He described Hitler as a madman, but said he deserved credit for building a strong state.

The Balkans

So much has been written about Slobodan Miloševic, now on trial for war crimes in the former Yugoslavia, that it would be pointless to repeat the obvious facts of his career here. Nonetheless, although he rose through the ranks of Yugoslavia's communist party, he was in a sense the most prominent 'far right' leader in Europe's recent history. I will restrict myself here to looking at why he comes as close as any leader to the definition of modern-day fascism — and demonstrates that there can be fascism of the left as well as of the right.

Misha Glenny wrote that Miloševic was the most paradoxical of dictators: 'He is a man without passion, without any real nationalist motivation (although on the surface he appears to wallow in it), and he is a man who has never shown any affection for the masses upon whom he depends for support.'[1] Overt nationalism and the active participation of the masses in politics were taboos in Tito's Yugoslavia, but Miloševic was to smash both in his pursuit of power. The Serb minority in Kosovo became his instrument to fan nationalist sentiments. It was Miloševic's speech there in 1989, championing their rights, that first stirred the dormant passions of Serb patriots and set the course towards building a 'Greater Serbia' which would include Serbs (and their territories) in other republics of Yugoslavia as it disintegrated into its constituent parts — Slovenia, Croatia, Bosnia-Herzegovina, Macedonia. Miloševic's chauvinism started a vicious circle: it revived, as a backlash, long-forgotten nationalist sentiments among the Slovenes, Croats and Bosnians (and the Croatian leader, Franjo Tudjman, in particular, was no slouch in playing the Croatian nationalist card); they created their own independent states, breaking away from Serbia but taking with them the Serb minorities scattered throughout the former Yugoslavia; and that in turn gave Miloševic the excuse he needed for territorial expansion (either directly or through proxies such as Radovan Karadzic, the leader of Bosnia's Serbs) to 'protect' those minorities... which, of course, further stoked the nationalism of the other nations, causing the downward spiral into the terrible Balkan wars of the nineties.

To achieve his territorial aims, Milošević needed the support of 'the masses'. Rhetoric alone was not enough to fuel their nationalism: he organised huge demonstrations in Serbia, Kosovo and the Vojvodina (home to a substantial Hungarian minority), to which unemployed people were paid to travel, in order to encourage hysteria and intimidate non-Serbs. The above-mentioned mass rally in 1989, at Kosovo's Field of Blackbirds, was the apotheosis of this — a choreographed celebration of Serb history, nationhood and glory, at which Milošević presented himself as the saviour of the nation. It was an event worthy of any of Europe's twentieth-century dictators, Hitler, Mussolini or Stalin.

Milošević's ultra-nationalist fanaticism and hatred led quite logically to the crimes for which he was put on trial by the International War Crimes Tribunal in the Hague — ethnic cleansing and genocide. It was his army that levelled the city of Vukovar in Croatia, expelling or massacring its population. It was his client Bosnian Serb army that 'cleansed' huge portions of Bosnia of non-Serbs, and carried out the single most brutal act of mass murder in Europe since the Second World War, when more than 7,000 men from the Muslim town of Srebrenica were rounded up, separated from their families and killed. The wars started by Milošević changed the ethnic balance of the former Yugoslavia, probably irrevocably. Some 1.3 million people remain displaced from their original homes.

But there were other, less violent, aspects of Miloševic's fascism. He fixed elections, altered constitutions and shifted from the Serbian presidency to the Yugoslav, to ensure he remained paramount leader and stayed in office. His toleration of other parties provided only a veneer of democracy. He controlled much of the media and employed paramilitary thugs. His contempt for other nations, indeed for human beings, was demonstrated at his trial, where he cleverly talked his way around laws he had introduced to suppress Albanian language and culture in Kosovo, citing texts to the letter to prove Albanians had all the freedom they needed — in much the way that Soviet dictators could 'prove' (by quoting weasel-worded laws and constitutions) that citizens in the one-party state participated in elections that were freer than in any western democracy.

Of all the politicians in this book, Miloševic was the ultimate preacher of hate. His own epitaph is written across tens of thousands of white stones that litter the green hills of Bosnia and Croatia — huge clusters of them on the outskirts of Sarajevo, in Vukovar, on the hillside above Srebrenica, every grave a reminder of the dangers of ultra-nationalism.

Notes

1 Misha Glenny, *The Fall of Yugoslavia*, London: Penguin, 1996, p. 31.

11.

The Mainstreaming of Far Right Politics

Politics at the end of the Millennium

In the early nineties, it seemed that the end of the Cold War had brought about what Francis Fukuyama called the 'end of history': the great clash of political systems had climaxed with the collapse of communism and the ultimate and irreversible triumph of capitalist markets and liberal politics. Journalists who had covered those remarkable years certainly felt they would never witness such seismic upheavals again.

I remember a poignant meeting with ex-President Mikhail Gorbachev a year or so after he was forced from power. At the end of our television interview he stood around in his office, waiting for us to tidy away our equipment, shuffling papers on his desk, chatting about this and that. The former president of the USSR, the man who had changed the face of Europe, now cut a sad and impotent figure. At one point he grew animated and grabbed a copy of some newspaper, pointing out something he strongly objected to; then he seemed to realise his anger was all a bit pointless, and he calmed down, packed up his briefcase, then ushered us out and switched off the light. It certainly seemed to me like the end of history.

But it wasn't. Life did not stand still in the last decade of the twentieth century. While the old East-West fault-line fused together, and the political systems on either side slowly converged, new pressures built up underground. They finally erupted spectacularly like a chain of volcanoes across the map of Europe — from Vienna to Rome, from Paris to Rotterdam and Copenhagen — as the far right triumphed and rocked the political Establishment. If this was Europe's new front line, it was a confused and diffuse one. Unlike the ideological divide of the post-War years, which split a continent, the new front cut through societies and communities. Each country had its own variety of far-right politician, but all of them thrived on the uncertainty caused by a major change of circumstances that occurred, inside and outside of Europe, during that lull when, it seemed, history had gone quiet.

One of those circumstances was the significant migration of people fleeing wars, oppression and poverty for the safety and prosperity of Europe. The figures were exaggerated by politicians who stood to gain by doing so: the influx was often portrayed as calamitous, both because of its 'huge' scale and because most of the refugees were neither white nor Christian. In fact, in the decade from 1992 to 2001, just over 4 million people applied for asylum in European countries whose total population is 484 million. Even if you double the figure to take account of illegal immigrants, it hardly amounts to a tidal wave — it is the equivalent of a school with 600 pupils taking in one foreigner each year. Of course, it did not happen like that: they did not disperse evenly all over Europe, but gravitated towards certain countries and certain cities, and these became the focus both of public discontent and political opportunism.

At the same time, the continent itself was rearranging its political furniture. In the east, former communist countries quickly threw off Soviet-imposed political and economic systems, but struggled to rebuild new ones. The prospect of joining NATO and the European Union helped them focus their minds on the task, as well as tempering some of their nationalistic excesses. The EU itself, meanwhile, not only prepared to let the new members in — without, incidentally, ever asking the existing family whether they wanted a new set of close, and poor, cousins — but also embarked on a series of reforms that shifted more and more power from national capitals to 'Brussels'. Brussels itself — in the sense of the European Commission, the EU's executive and civil service — did not in fact receive any more power, but the community did. Governments, in other words, chose to share sovereignty increasingly with the other member states. More and more areas of policy were brought within the EU's ambit, starting with the single market, leading to the single currency, and adding common foreign, security and defence policies, until a situation arose where the vast majority of national legislation had to be made in conformity with EU directives, or in consultation with EU allies. Even though the directly elected European Parliament became joint-legislator (together with the fifteen member states' governments) in almost all areas, it remained a remote, poorly understood and mistrusted body. Indeed, the Union itself was a baffling construct to almost all of its citizens. The more powers it gained, the more threatening it seemed. And the more it was 'democratised' — by, for example, involving the parliament in additional policy areas — the more complex and confusing it all became. Its self-destructing capacity reached near-fulfilment with the Treaty of Nice, agreed in December 2000: intended to 'streamline' decision-making, it in fact

complicated it to an astonishing degree. Henceforth —
imagine this! — all legislation would be adopted by adding
up the votes of member states (weighted according to their
populations), but subject to three different types of
threshold, double qualified majority and blocking
minority — ensuring that in future only mathematics
professors would really understand how any given EU
policy came to be adopted or rejected. And that is just in
the 'council of ministers' (summits or ministerial-level
meetings of the fifteen member states): most directives *also*
have to be approved by the parliament — not forgetting
the Commission's pennyworth in drafting and implementing them. Compare all that to the simple show of
hands, electronic vote or division-lobby of a national
parliament. No wonder the decade saw a waning of
support for the Union, as it was sucked inexorably into a
whirlpool of its own devising. No wonder the far right
found it so easy to add anti-EU sentiment to its arsenal.

This was not the only way in which mainstream politics
lost its appeal in the late twentieth century. In several
countries the radical right, epitomised by Margaret
Thatcher in Britain and Ronald Reagan in the US, had held
sway for many years, and credited itself with having
brought down communism. But the mid-nineties brought
a backlash to their brand of ultra-free-market economics
and uncaring, sink-or-swim social policies. Bill Clinton,
Tony Blair and Gerhard Schröder rose on the tide.

However, this was not a reversion to old-style socialism, but 'the third way'. For Blair it was 'New Labour', for Schröder it was '*die neue Mitte*' (the new centre), in both cases a symbiosis of right-wing or liberal economics and leftish social policies. France had already stumbled towards a similar outcome, with its cohabitation of a socialist prime minister and right-of-centre president. Most other countries in western Europe were there already: they had had right-left coalitions, with thriving economies and bountiful welfare states, for years. By the end of the millennium, it looked as though Europe had achieved the ultimate healing of post-cold-war wounds. The 'Left' (but really the centre) was in power in almost every EU member state, while eastern European nations ten years on from communism were poised to cross the threshold and join them.

What nobody expected was that this beautiful third way might spell the death of politics. After all, if government was now so inclusive and broad, who needed opposition, who needed dissent? Elections became boring, as middle-of-the-road parties offered scarcely-differing agendas. In Britain and Germany the centre-right opposition parties disintegrated into squabbling: how do you oppose a government when you agree with half of what it is doing? France had its Jospin-Chirac double act. The rest of Europe had centre-left prime ministers in charge of a variety of 'Olive Tree', 'rainbow', purple-green, red-black, and other pick'n'mix coalitions. As a result, election turnouts collapsed, while viewing figures for Big Brother soared, all across the continent. It was the triumph of anti-politics — a major factor in the growth of the far right.

The rebellion against traditional politics was also encouraged by the perceived growth of sleaze among the political classes. In countries like Austria, Belgium and Italy the mainstream parties had practised a form of patronage or party-cronyism for decades, dividing up posts in the administration and public services between them. In France, a president was able to stand for re-election despite a clamour of disgust at his alleged corruption, while in Italy a man facing multiple criminal charges became prime minister.

So of course, this was not the end of history at all. The seismic activity had not stopped: it had just shifted to find new weak points in Europe's political landscape. While above ground the 'new centre' and old coalitions pressed on with bland policies acceptable to a broad, middle-of-the-road constituency, there was a rumbling deep below, where resentments and worries and fears had been pushed, out of sight. While above ground, political correctness held sway, below the surface frustration was growing at the inability to speak out. A small but growing number of people, in most European countries, wanted to break the taboos and smash the complacency of the Establishment. In several of them, demagogues and populists were waiting to become their mouthpiece. At the turn of the millennium Jörg Haider became the first of them to break through, starting a trend that within a couple of years changed the face of European politics.

Racism and Islam

The factors outlined above — immigration, EU integration, centrist politics and corruption — provided a common compost for the growth of far-right politics in western Europe. Immigration encouraged xenophobia, integration fostered nationalism, institutionalised centrism encouraged both apathy and extremism, and sleaze left the field open for populists proposing to 'clean things up'. These elements did not come together uniformly in the various parties described in this book. Indeed, what should be clear is their great diversity, in terms of their roots, history, policies, impact and potential danger.

It is tempting to try to put the parties into categories, however loosely, in order to judge what they have in common and what separates them. At the 'soft' end of the spectrum are the Danish People's Party, Forza Italia and the Pim Fortuyn List, which may be described as populist and xenophobic (with the added complication, in Berlusconi's case, of unbridled corporate power dressed in a politician's suit). Then there are the more hardline far-right movements such as the Vlaams Blok, Le Pen's National Front, Haider's Freedom Party, the Northern League and the National Alliance in Italy, and Germany's DVU and Republikaner, which are generally nationalist and racist (as well as populist), sometimes authoritarian, and in some cases nostalgic for or indulgent towards their fascist or Nazi predecessors. And at the extreme end of the spectrum are parties which combine all the above qualities but are overtly neo-Nazi, support hanging and flogging, and have a violent skinhead following — for example, the British National Party and Germany's NPD.

One factor underlies all of these movements, however strenuously each would try to deny it: racism. This is seen, for example, in the fact that, although they are nationalistic, and therefore put *their own* nations first, the parties themselves for the most part regard each other as 'kindred' organisations. Several of the west European parties also maintain links with ultra-nationalists in Russia, Slovakia and elsewhere. So, paradoxically, while asserting the primacy of their own people, they are willing to include others in their political grouping. This suggests that the definition of 'own people first' is fairly broad — wide enough to include other Europeans, at least. In other words, the slogan is a cover for '*white* people first' — an attempt to conceal the essential racism of all of these groups. In Belgium, Filip Dewinter speaks openly of defending not just his own Flemish nation but the

European nation, and describes his allies as 'right nationalist' parties. Some of these parties have formal links — a process which Jörg Haider is eager to promote. In July 2002 he held a 'summit' in Carinthia with Dewinter and the Vlaams Blok chairman, Frank Vanhecke, and a former MEP for Italy's Northern League, Mario Borghesia. They discussed proposals to set up a common far-right list of candidates for the European Parliament elections in 2004.

Racism, or xenophobia, is the rationale behind the far right's anti-immigration campaigns, behind its welfare chauvinism (the 'national preference' or however else it is described), and also behind its demands for law and order, for politicians like Pia Kjaersgaard, Jean-Marie Le Pen or Filip Dewinter make no secret of their belief that rising crime rates are due primarily to immigrants. It would be wrong to say there is *no* correlation: crime *is* higher in many immigrant communities — but so are unemployment, poverty and other social problems. The far right politicians, however, make little attempt to understand the causes of crime, rather they seek to solve it merely by scapegoating immigrants.

Racism forms the bedrock of these politicians' philosophy. They share a fundamental belief in the superiority of their own nations, and, by extension, of the European race. I have not attempted to give a precise definition of 'fascism' in this book, preferring to explore the specific manifestations of different far-right politicians' views, but if one were to look for an obvious element of 'neo-fascism' here, then this would be it.[1] And, as I will argue later in this chapter, it is precisely this element of the far-right agenda which has been hijacked by the political mainstream.

Racist attitudes, particularly regarding Muslims, increased perceptibly following the September 11th attacks. The press in most countries contributed to this by their constant repetition of the phrase 'Islamic fundamentalist' to describe Osama Bin Laden and the Al-Qaida terrorist network, even though many Muslims would argue that there is nothing 'fundamentally Islamic' about these or any other terrorists — indeed that Islam is fundamentally opposed to terrorism. Newspapers which would never dream of calling the bombers of the Irish Republican Army 'Christian fundamentalists' saw nothing wrong with using a religious term to describe the madmen who flew passenger planes into the World Trade Centre, thereby denigrating an entire religion in the eyes of many readers. Even broadcasters such as the BBC, which strive for impartiality, and have severe qualms over using the word 'terrorist' (even when describing an act of political violence demonstrably aimed at civilians), used the phrase 'Islamic fundamentalist' without compunction — almost as a synonym for terrorist. This undoubtedly reinforced prejudices against Muslims in general, and caused widespread unease among ordinary, peaceful Muslims who had nothing but contempt for the terrorists who carried out terrible crimes supposedly in the name of their religion.

The unconscious link between 'terrorism' and 'Islam' was strengthened in the year after the New York attacks by constant reiteration as part of President George W. Bush's 'war on terror', which was aimed exclusively at Islamic countries and organisations. The link looked likely to be strengthened if the US went ahead with its plans to attack Iraq and oust its leader, Saddam Hussein. Arab leaders warned of 'chaos across the region'. 'If you strike Iraq, and kill the people of Iraq while Palestinians are being killed in Israel,' said President Mubarak of Egypt, 'not one Arab leader will be able to control the angry outburst of the masses... I do not think there is one Arab state that wants a strike on Iraq — not Kuwait, not Saudi Arabia, not any other state.'[2] The scene was thus set for a further polarisation, with the Arab world against the European/American world. In terms of European politics, it suggested that anti-Islamic, and anti-Arab, feeling would grow stronger, fostered by right-wing newspapers and politicians, and feeding into increased support for extremist parties.

And yet, whatever the far right might think of them, millions of Muslims live in Europe — more than 4 million in France, more than 3 million in Germany, and as many as 1.3 million in Britain — and the vast majority of them are not crazy suicide-bombers, but ordinary, peaceful folk, who respect the laws of the countries in which they live and pose no danger whatsoever to liberal, democratic values. Most are hard-working: it would be interesting to know how the bovver-boys of the British National Party would feel without their local curry house or handy Asian corner-shop, open till all hours.

There are three possibilities for co-existence: a multicultural society, in which Muslims freely practise their religion, speak their own languages and keep their own cultures; integration, by which they keep their distinct identity but become part of the 'host' community; and assimilation, by which they lose all traces of their original identity, including even their religion, and become indistinguishable from their 'host' nation, apart from the colour of their skin. The last option is the one preferred by almost all the far-right politicians discussed in this book, not just the Fortuyns, Le Pens and Dewinters, but even the 'more moderate' populists of the Danish variety. Multiculturalism can pose problems, there is no doubt, as it encourages immigrant communities to stick together — and therefore isolated from the 'outside' community. By failing to learn the country's language well, they not only attract discrimination but also find it harder to get jobs — leading to poverty and a further withdrawal into their own closed world. But there is no reason why immigrants cannot retain their customs, traditions, religion, and even language (so long as they also learn their new country's tongue), and still integrate well into the community at large. A diversity of cultures does not have to disrupt society: it can enrich it. This has been demonstrated amply by previous generations of well-integrated Caribbean and Asian people in Britain, for example, and the same can doubtless happen with the latest influx of immigrants — if they are given the chance, with positive measures taken to promote employment and outlaw discrimination. And of course, the immigrants themselves must wish to be integrated: certain Islamist groups regard integration into Western societies as treason, but then, one wonders, why come to Europe in the first place?

No one should pretend it is easy. It is perfectly natural and right for Europeans to be shocked and outraged by legal practices in certain Islamic countries, where thieves' limbs are amputated and women are stoned to death for adultery. It is hardly surprising if news of such events — not to mention the issuing of fatwas against writers or the planning of terrorist attacks against civilians, or the preaching of hate-filled sermons by certain imams — raises the hackles of most Europeans. But then, barbarism presumably horrifies the majority of Muslims who have chosen to live in Europe too. The evil of the far right is that it does not distinguish between the zealots and the ordinary person who has come to Europe in search of a new life.

The Rise of the Far Right

There is a more measured alternative to the right's blanket condemnation of Islam as a 'backward' religion, incompatible with European life. The left-leaning German foreign minister, Joschka Fischer, for example, called for a study into whether Islamic traditions and teachings were compatible with the values of modern Western societies. In Holland, the government is considering whether imams practising in Europe could be encouraged to adopt western values on such matters as homosexuality or women's rights. There is a wider debate on whether a 'European version' of Islam is possible. This would presumably permit complete freedom to follow the religion, while weeding out any practices which contravene European law, such as incitement to violence. Whether or not this eventually happens, Muslims already live in Europe in great numbers, and more will come. That is only a problem so long as intolerance — on both sides — exists.

The Far Right's Varied Success

Far-right parties have taken root — or sprung from older roots — to a varied extent in different countries. Britain and Germany have proved most resistant to their challenge, notwithstanding an alarming level of neo-Nazi violence in Germany and to a lesser extent in England. This may be because in both countries the far-right parties are more overtly fascist than elsewhere, and are therefore considered beyond the pale by most citizens. The parties here also suffer from poor leadership and lack of access to sympathetic media outlets. The electoral systems undoubtedly play a part: in Britain the first-past-the-post system eliminates small parties, and in Germany the threshold of 5 per cent to win seats in the Bundestag has the same effect. In Germany, of course, the burden of the Nazi past ensures that far-right parties have limited appeal, and the state has pursued an active policy of suppressing and infiltrating them (though, to be sure, its crass attempts to infiltrate the NPD have severely jeopardised its moves to ban it). In Britain, the far right's fortunes have varied somewhat according to how right-wing the government of the day is: under Mrs Thatcher's right-wing government, the popularity of the National Front waned, and while the British National Party has had a small breakthrough since Labour returned to power, it remains insignificant and may be further undermined by Labour's own tough line on immigration. In both countries 'anti-politics', in the sense of a reaction to bland consensus politics, and to the political distribution of jobs in the state apparatus, is less of a factor: Britain's civil service is politically neutral, and voting Labour or Conservative can bring about real swings in policy, while in Germany, too, governments have changed substantially as a result of elections, despite the presence of a small party (Liberal or Green) in most coalitions.

In all the other countries considered here the far-right parties may be better described as populist and nationalist than neo-fascist, and all have made great efforts to present themselves as respectable democratic movements. Most of them have succeeded by persuading voters that nationalism is an acceptable belief, even when tainted with racism. In Belgium the Vlaams Blok portrays itself as a victim — kept out of power by an unholy alliance of parties which ignore the threat to the Flemish nation; the Danish People's Party has achieved the accolade of being not just tolerated in parliament but relied upon to pass laws — including an immigration law much to its liking; the Austrian Freedom Party signed a 'declaration' stating its adherence to European values; Pim Fortuyn sought respectability by presenting his anti-Islamic policies as 'pro-European' and 'pro-democracy'.

Jean-Marie Le Pen's success is perhaps the greatest mystery. He has never concealed his xenophobia, indeed, he flaunted it. Yet he defied an electoral system that normally keeps extreme parties out and ensures that a centre-right and a centre-left candidate go through to the final round of voting by overtaking one of those candidates and coming second himself. Alone among the successful far-right politicians, rather than trying to appear moderate or respectable, Le Pen revelled, perhaps, in his notoriety and unashamed populism. The whole thrust of his appeal was as a man willing publicly to call Chirac corrupt, and to offer simple, direct solutions to crime, excessive immigration and Brussels domination. It is interesting that Le Pen is the only far-right European politician with whom the others are somewhat ashamed (at least in public) to be associated. When I asked Filip Dewinter about the attempts being made to forge a Europe-wide 'right-wing nationalist' party, he mentioned all of them apart from Le Pen. When I pushed him on this he admitted it was because, while he personally had no problem with him, 'I think for the Austrians, and for other [far-right] parties who are in power now, it will be difficult — he is a little bit too extreme. It will take some time before we can make one big right-wing nationalist party including Le Pen.'

The rise of ultra-nationalism in former communist countries may be attributed partly to a lack of western values — paradoxically a lack of precisely the kind of 'political correctness' that fuels the rise of the far-right in western Europe. One commentator, for example, posited that it was the absence of a culture of political correctness in eastern Germany that made it a breeding ground for extremist groups: 'East Germany lacks a generally accepted foundation of values, whereas West Germany acquired its values over a long process. [Through a series of major debates over the decades] West Germans agreed the rules by which conflicts are carried out. Generally accepted convictions were arrived at democratically. At any rate, anyone who contradicts the consensus of values can expect to be disapproved of or even shunned. In the West political correctness outlaws open xenophobia — whereas in East Germany tolerance in itself is not a value.'[3] The same goes for many east European countries, where the collapse of a state-enforced 'socialist morality', which had excluded all normal debate about human values, left an ethical void. Russia is a prime example of this: deprived for seven decades (indeed, several centuries) of meaningful debate about society, nationality, racism or human rights, there is no culture of social morality to counter the streak of bigotry that runs through all levels of society. Anti-Semitism is considerably weaker than it used to be, but it has been replaced by an increasingly virulent form of xenophobia targeted against dark-skinned people from the Caucasian republics and central Asia. Both East Germany and Russia suffer from the disorientation of a communist society which allegedly taught 'enlightened' values but in fact undermined them by the brutality of the state itself.

But in western Europe political correctness is now used as a pejorative term by far-right parties who blame it for covering up burning issues. The race factor in crime is a good example. Police forces prefer not to issue statistics broken down by race, because it is considered discriminatory. But far from making the issue go away, it turned it into a subject for uninformed gossip and speculation — just what populists need to bolster people's prejudices. It made it more difficult to tackle the causes of crimes committed by immigrants (since the statistics were not readily available) while allowing people's fears and insecurities to proliferate out of ignorance. Thus, it was a release for the people of Rotterdam when Pim Fortuyn broke that 'taboo' — but instead of it being a constructive release of energy, directed at solving the causes of crime, it simply released pent-up prejudices, allowing people to advocate the simplest of solutions: 'Keep the foreigners out!'

Other Countries

'Success', for Europe's far right parties, is measured by the extent to which they are accepted into the mainstream of politics, blurring the distinction between hard and centre right. By that standard, Berlusconi has been spectacularly successful: he and his more extreme partners assumed power with scarcely a murmur of discontent heard from other European capitals — Bill Clinton and Tony Blair even joined him for a pop charity recording. Fortuyn and Haider came next in the 'success table' of the far right, as their colleagues were accepted as government ministers, albeit with misgivings abroad. In France, Le Pen won the votes of a large section of the public, and some of his party colleagues took power in major cities, whereas the Vlaams Blok, despite a high share of the vote, remained locked out of the mainstream by the *cordon sanitaire*. If indirect influence was also a measure, then Britain's BNP would be happy that the Labour government was implementing harsher immigration policies. There are other countries in Europe, too, not so far mentioned in this book, where the far right has done well: Switzerland, Norway and Portugal.

Switzerland, which prides itself on its neutrality, humanity and ancient form of democracy by referendum, has long suffered from xenophobia. As long ago as 1974, when I spent a year there as a student, a referendum was held on restricting the numbers of foreign workers. I remember protesting pathetically to a waiter who wanted to throw me and an American friend out of the famous café Odeon in Zurich, apparently just because we were foreign: 'Hah,' I said, 'so it's true what they say about Swiss xenophobia!'

To be fair, Switzerland was by far the most generous country in the world when it came to receiving refugees in the nineties. It took in almost four times as many as Britain, per head of population. The peak year was 1999, when 46,000 — mainly Albanians from Kosovo — applied for asylum. Housed in camps all over this small country, their presence was unmissable. A journalist visiting the village of Hitzkirch, in the heart of German-speaking Switzerland, near Lucerne, found local people had a real sense of being overwhelmed by the Kosovo refugees. One woman said the younger generation was more afraid of foreigners than the older one: 'These feelings are not against foreigners in general but primarily against the Albanians because there are so many of them in the schools and they behave like little kings in their leather jackets.' A local journalist said the women and children were made to feel more welcome than the men: 'People are very aggressive towards them. They say, "Why don't you go back now? NATO has bombed your country free. You have to repair your houses. What are you doing here?"'[4]

It can scarcely be a coincidence that in October that year, just three weeks after Jörg Haider's success in neighbouring Austria, the anti-immigration Swiss People's Party (*Schweizerische Volkspartei* or SVP) achieved a massive swing to the right and took the largest share of the vote in a Swiss general election. Its millionaire leader, Christoph Blocher, targeted the two big fears of many Swiss — foreigners and the European Union, which Switzerland has been toying with joining for years. But he also tapped into latent anti-Semitism which was aroused in the late nineties by the World Jewish Congress's fight for Holocaust reparations from Swiss banks. Blocher called it 'pure extortion'.

Is Blocher really to be feared, though? Probably not. He is a populist but no fascist, and his calls for an end to immigration are not new in Switzerland (nor unusual in

Europe generally these days). In any case, no major decisions in this country are taken by a single man or even by a single party: they are not even taken by the government (and Blocher's party has just one seat in the seven-member cabinet), but by the Swiss people in referendums. And there is still a very large majority of Swiss people who did not vote for Blocher.

*

In Scandinavia, Sweden has remained a model of moderation: here the far right has made less headway than anywhere in Europe. Norway's anti-immigration Progress Party, however, emulated the success of the Danish People's Party by securing 26 seats in the 165-member parliament at the last election, in September 2001. Like its Danish counterpart, it holds the balance of power — it is not a member of the centre-right coalition but its votes are required for legislation to be passed. This situation gives it extraordinary power. For example, it made a deal with two opposition parties, the Socialist Left and the Labour Party, to increase government funding of nursery places, and forced this through parliament. The Christian Democrat-led government opposed the bill but will have to implement it when it enters into force in 2004.

The nursery scheme illustrates the 'social agenda' that many populist parties of the right combine with their better-known strategies on immigration and crime. The Progress Party, led by the charismatic Carl I. Hagen ('King Carl'), proposed capping immigration at one thousand a year (in 2001 there were 14,780 asylum seekers), and repatriating those who broke the law. Hagen advocates abolishing development aid to the third world because he believes the money is used to buy 'arms and luxury goods' or is squandered by inefficient regimes. At home, Hagen, who in the early seventies demanded welfare cuts, now wants Norway's prodigious North Sea oil and gas revenue to be spent on things like public health and care for the elderly. It is this issue rather than immigration that has persuaded many left-leaning voters to desert the social democrats and vote for the Progress Party.

Both his party and Pia Kjaersgaard's People's Party in Denmark have been described as less extreme versions of, say, Le Pen's National Front, related to it in the way that social democrats are related to communists: 'It is perhaps only to be expected that, in social-democratic Scandinavia, we find less extreme (or more "social democratic") variants of this new type of party.'[5] It may be rather kind, however, to suggest that parties whose world-outlook is basically racist are the 'social democrats' of the right: I would suggest they are more dangerous than that, even if they espouse a number of social causes which would also appeal to left-wing voters.

The Iberian peninsula, like Scandinavia, is divided. Spain, arguably because of its long and relatively recent experience of Franco's fascist dictatorship (1936-75), has no prominent extreme-right party (though nationalist parties thrive in the Basque country and Catalonia). On the other hand, Portugal's long and recent experience of dictatorship (1932-74) has not prevented the entry of the anti-immigrant, anti-EU *Partido Popular* (Popular Party) into government. Under the leadership of a young lawyer, Paulo Portas, it gained only 8.8 per cent of the vote (14 seats) in the 2002 general election but joined a coalition with the oddly-named 'Social Democrats' (in fact a centre-right party), ending six years of socialist government. Portas himself became defence minister.

The Popular Party's manifesto included not only 'predictable' populist demands for tight limits on immigration, lowering the age at which young people could be jailed and an end to the transfer of more powers to the EU, but also a demand that all schoolchildren should sing the national anthem every day. It talked of a 'climate of uncertainty' in the cities, because of immigrant-linked crime, and praised Portuguese colonial rule as the 'foundation stone of civilisation and values'. Its influence remains limited, however.

The Mainstream Response

The far right's first major success, in Austria, met with a forthright but misguided response from other EU nations. Prompted by a rash Portuguese socialist government, which then held the rotating presidency of the Union, and cheered on by France and Belgium, they imposed diplomatic sanctions which backfired by fuelling anti-EU sentiment in Austria, and were in any case exaggerated and unnecessary. Israel's recall of its ambassador to Vienna and advice to Austrian Jews to leave the country — almost as if Hitler himself had returned — was absurd.

Later, as other populists scored victories or came to office, this did not happen — not even for Berlusconi, arguably a much greater threat to democracy than Haider. This may have been due to lack of principle — pushing little Austria around was one thing, but Italy was too big a fish — but it was also because the EU had learnt its lesson and did not want to burn its fingers again. By the time the People's Party acquired its key position in the Danish parliament, there was no reaction whatsoever. And Fortuyn's posthumous victory generated much heat but no fire. As for Le Pen, the reaction abroad to his triumph in the first round of the French presidential election was tumultuous: newspapers devoted screeds to it, politicians boldly denounced him, apparently casting aside all doubts about the morality of interfering in another country's democratic process. But these were cheap shots: everyone knew they were attacking a loser, that they would never have to impose sanctions or any other measures against France because it was evident that Le Pen could not possibly win in the second round. It was a chance to protest loudly while knowing that words would never have to be turned into action.

By now Europe had in any case moved on from the kind of socialist-dominated camp which had denounced Haider in 1999. In the space of about two years a great swing of the pendulum replaced centre-left governments with centre-right ones in many countries. Austria was first to go (with the conservative Wolfgang Schüssel replacing the social democratic chancellor, Viktor Klima); in Spain the conservative José Maria Aznar was re-elected in March 2000; then Italy, Denmark, Portugal, Holland, and finally France fell to the right. Belgium and Finland had broad 'rainbow coalitions' led by Liberals and Social Democrats respectively. Nominally left-wing governments remained in power only in Sweden, Greece, Britain and Germany (Chancellor Schröder having narrowly faced off the right-wing challenge of Edmund Stoiber in the autumn of 2002).

Many of the new governing parties, as we have seen, gained support by openly copying far-right policies on crime and immigration — and even in Britain and Belgium the centrist governments are acting just as 'tough' as the right-wingers, leaving Göran Persson's Swedish government fighting a lonely battle on the left. He and the then socialist French government, for example, were alone in opposing EU plans to punish third world countries which refused to take back rejected asylum seekers by fining them or depriving them of development aid.

This was the new reality — and in a way the ultimate victory of the populists. Without having to get their hands dirty by actually governing, they were seeing many of their most reactionary policies implemented by mainstream parties. Compassion seemed to have deserted Europe, as its governments vied with each other to be the toughest on illegal — and even legal — immigration. The rhetoric reached fever pitch, with Britain's home secretary talking of 'swamping' by foreigners and Italy's Umberto Bossi threatening to blow refugee ships out of the water. First Denmark, then Italy, then Holland and Spain introduced draconian measures to dissuade asylum seekers from even trying. In Britain, Downing Street mooted the possibility of warships patrolling Europe's shores to intercept people traffickers, and bulk deportations of illegal immigrants on RAF transport planes. The suggestion by Blair and Aznar that aid to developing countries be made conditional on them stemming the flow was rejected as nonsensical by the European Commission. The commissioner for development, Poul Nielson, said: 'It makes no sense to link development assistance to a country's performance on migration. Sanctions would be counterproductive and meaningless.' There was no question, he said, of depriving countries like Somalia — a source of large-scale migration — of humanitarian aid. Withdrawal of aid would only hurt the poorer sections of society, and thereby encourage even more emigration. Blair's stance was so tough that Europe's right-wing governments took to citing him as evidence that their own policies were more moderate than they might seem.

The European Commission itself was spurred into a rush of activity to finalise a common policy on asylum and immigration which had been on a variety of drawing boards for years. But it was outstripped by the haste of member states to tighten up their own procedures. 'Fortress Europe' beckoned. As EU leaders met in Seville in June 2002 Amnesty International issued an urgent appeal to them not to trample on human rights in their haste to fight illegal immigration. 'Fear appears to be the driving force. Fear on the part of citizens about the effects of the perceived abuse of the asylum system on their economic, social and security conditions. Fear on the part of governments that the extreme or even not so extreme right will cash in politically. Fear of the alien, fear of losing grip. Fear is not a good basis for making policy. Facts dissolve, perceptions and simplifications reign, racist prejudice breeds.'[6]

'It defies rationality,' wrote one British commentator, 'yet it has become the most salient political fact in contemporary Europe. Numbers of legal and illegal immigrants may be falling; Europe may need many more to sustain its working population; and cities like London may owe their vibrancy to the jostling energy of so many cultures and ethnic groups. But Europe's political establishment is running scared. European governments are in an unseemly competition to put up barriers and reassure electorates that the supply lines of alien "others" are being shut down.'[7]

Apart from Sweden, only Germany stood out as something of an exception. Perhaps because of its guilt complex associated with its treatment of non-Germans during the Nazi period, it opened its doors to nearly 80 per cent of those seeking asylum in the EU during the early nineties. One of the first and most audacious acts of the Schröder government in 1998 was to offer the possibility of German citizenship to millions of Turkish and other *Gastarbeiter* — the people who had stoked the country's economic miracle with their cheap labour and decided to stay. The law ended the practice of granting citizenship only to those who could prove German ancestry. Schröder also gave the 35,000 Muslim children in Berlin the right to Islamic religious education. And finally, in 2002 (even as the anti-immigrant clamour resounded around Europe) the government passed its new immigration law, designed to entice skilled workers into the country — dispelling the notion that all immigrants are spongers and uneducated.

These were lonely voices. For the most part mainstream political parties across the continent had intentionally adopted a hard line as their strategy to defeat the far-right threat — not by telling them they were wrong, but by occupying their territory. No one, apart from the United Nations Refugee Agency and some human rights and welfare organisations, argued against it. Politicians of almost every shade seemed to be convinced that even to hint to voters that immigration might have its positive side, that foreigners were not all lazy, uneducated and crooked, and that compassion was a virtue worth clinging to, was the surest way to lose an election.

Blip or Danger?

So are we really witnessing a 'march of the far right'? Are we really entering a new Dark Age? Or is this a historic blip?

There has been no shortage of alarmist talk, with suggestions that Europe is 'sliding into an abyss', and that the threat of racism and fascism is greater than at any time since the thirties.[8]

Certainly, the lessons of the thirties have to be taken seriously. One: Hitler's party was a 'National Socialist' party, combining, as do many of today's far-right movements, ultra-nationalism and xenophobia with superficially left-wing projects, aimed at protecting the man on the street and providing state-funded benefits (a Volkswagen for every citizen). Two: the Nazis tempered their language at strategic moments, and built up their position of power gradually — exploiting opportunities that presented themselves, using democratic elections, and partly concealing their true nature until they were in an unassailable position. Few observers in the twenties foresaw how the party's policies and electoral appeal would develop.

Vigilance, then, is not out of place. Yet having said that, I believe that the threat today is more of a descent into illiberality than of a return to thirties-style fascism. As far as one can foresee at present, there will be no jackboots and Nuremberg rallies, but a steady and insidious erosion of the ideals of European society, with old prejudices revived and the values of tolerance and enlightenment debased.

There will be no return of the jackboot because none of the far right parties with any influence in Europe is a fascist party of that type, at least as far as one can judge by their activities to date. (I exclude, in other words, the small and uninfluential neo-Nazi groups.) Even those parties which try to play according to democratic rules — the majority of those examined in this book — are largely kept from real power by a variety of means. In Belgium there is the *cordon sanitaire* (though a similar 'quarantine' was broken in Austria by the Freedom Party). In other countries there are electoral thresholds to be crossed. Even in France, Le Pen's disturbingly high vote in the end won him no power whatsoever (and let us not forget that his vote actually increased only marginally from the previous election). Those far-right parties which have managed to secure seats in a coalition government (in Austria, Holland) have tended to be 'tamed' by the experience. The very fact of working in a democratic parliament — and in a democratic Europe — has forced them to soften their language. Italy's tainted triumvirate is an explosive cocktail of neo-fascism, racism and the unscrupulous mixing of business and politics — but even it remains subject to EU laws and peer pressure. Several of the parties (Pim Fortuyn's, Jörg Haider's) are squabbling and may be past their peak.

This is not to say the populists are not a menace. Parties like the Danish People's Party may not be 'extremist' but they are imbued with an unpleasant ultra-nationalist and therefore xenophobic ideology. The measures they advocate, and indeed introduce where they have succeeded in joining government, play to a mean-minded public gallery. They are not *dangerous*, in the sense of threatening democracy or other countries. They have no fascist militaristic agenda. They do not threaten to close down other parties. But they are dangerous in another sense. Populism means speaking the language of the man on the street, freely expressing attitudes which more politically correct politicians avoid, even though they have strong popular support. That can have deeply disturbing consequences — in society, by fostering an atmosphere of intolerance and making anti-democratic sentiments appear 'normal', and in politics by leading to legislation that may infringe the human or civil rights of large portions of the population, almost always defined by their race, colour or origins.

Political correctness, so derided by all the politicians of the far right, developed for a reason: it is the product of civilisation, and reflects a basic desire to tolerate, not persecute, those who have different faiths, beliefs, or skin colour. Where the populists have a point, though, is in saying that political correctness has prevented dispassionate or informed analysis of complex situations. A balance, surely, needs to be found, which would remove the appeal of extremists who 'dare to speak the truth' (but in fact merely mouth the prejudices of the public bar) while preserving the values of tolerance and acceptance that make modern civilisation the inclusive, welcoming society into which it has developed over centuries.

The wave of immigration that sparked so much anti-foreigner feeling over the past decade may not last for ever — indeed it is already waning — and that, together with the fact that European governments are themselves vocally and actively combating immigration, should lessen the impact of the far right. Other unforeseen crises, on the other hand — a catastrophic war in Iraq, an explosion of oil prices, an economic collapse, a fresh round of refugees — could once again make mainstream governments look ineffective and radical solutions attractive. That is the kind of situation that the far right is waiting for.

The extremists may or may not succeed in dragging us back to the Dark Ages, but Europe certainly needs to be on its guard. On its guard not just against the populists and demagogues themselves, but against those who now masquerade in their clothes while pretending to be liberal.

Notes

1 For a detailed discussion of definitions of fascism, see Richard Griffiths, *An Intelligent Person's Guide to Fascism*, London: Duckworth, 2000.

2 *The Times*, 28 August 2002.

3 *Die Zeit*, 15/1999.

4 Linda Grant in *The Guardian*, 5 November 1999.

5 Jørgen Goul Andersen and Tor Bjørklund, 'Radical Right-Wing Populism in Scandinavia', in P. Hainsworth, *op. cit.*, p. 220.

6 Amnesty International Open Letter to the Heads of State or Government of the European Union, 12 June 2002.

7 Will Hutton in *The Observer*, 9 June 2002.

8 See, for example, Martin Jacques, 'The new barbarism' in *The Guardian*, 9 May 2002.

Index

Index

Index

Index